Rebuilding Any

AUTOMOTIVE

Step-by-Step VIDEOBOOK™

Engine

Barry Kluczyk

CarTech®

CarTech®

CarTech,® Inc.
39966 Grand Avenue
North Branch, MN 55056
Phone: 651-277-1200 or 800-551-4754
Fax: 651-277-1203
www.cartechbooks.com

Edit by Paul Johnson
Layout by Monica Seiberlich

ISBN 978-1-934709-11-5
Item No. SA179

Printed in China
10 9 8 7 6 5 4 3 2 1

OVERSEAS DISTRIBUTION BY:

Brooklands Books Ltd.
P.O. Box 146, Cobham, Surrey, KT11 1LG, England
Telephone 01932 865051 • Fax 01932 868803
www.brooklands-books.com

Brooklands Books Aus.
3/37-39 Green Street, Banksmeadow, NSW 2019, Australia
Telephone 2 9695 7055 • Fax 2 9695 7355

CONTENTS

DEDICATION

This book is dedicated to my wife, Carrie, and daughter, Mary, who graciously put up with all my time in the garage and office during its production.

Thanks to Brian Thomson and his crew at Thomson Automotive in Redford, Michigan. They always accommodated my nosing into their work to shoot photos for this book and other projects. I appreciate it.

PREFACE

Engine rebuilding is a time-honored tradition and like so many vocations, pastimes, and institutions of the last century, it has seemingly gone the way of television repair, drive-in movies, or mom-and-pop hardware stores. It's easy to understand the reasons: contemporary automotive engines and their control systems are quite complex, creating the proverbial "plumbers nightmare" under the hood; ready-built replacement engines and crate engines are plentiful and cost-effective; and, modern engines are manufactured with better designs, materials, and methods that have drastically reduced the need for the traditional rebuild.

The evolution of society has something to do with it, too. A great many people live in suburban areas that don't afford much extra space for pulling an engine out of a car and rebuilding it on a nearby workbench. Besides, who has the time for such an endeavor? Long commutes and the myriad details of everyday life make it difficult to carve out the time for such a project.

To create this book, I made the time. Citing all the reasons mentioned above—lack of time in my daily schedule being the biggest factor—it would have been easy to order a replacement engine or simply send off my car to an engine shop for a complete rebuild. I did neither. Sure, the book project helped make the decision for me, but, like so many other enthusiasts, it was something I'd wanted to do for a long time. I may never climb a mountain, snorkel in the Caribbean, or win a Pulitzer Prize for my automotive writing, but I've torn down, rebuilt, and reinstalled an engine in my own car.

Of course, I relied on professionals for necessary machine work and a few other details that I was not equipped to handle at home. However, except for a stubborn exhaust system, I removed the engine. I tore it down. I re-assembled it with new parts. I measured all the necessary clearances and tolerances. I re-installed it in the car. And, most importantly, I got that rebuilt engine to start.

Few feelings of accomplishment compare to turning the ignition key after completing such a project and hearing, feeling, and seeing the fruits of the labor. It is a very satisfying experience, to say the least, and novices can accomplish it. The keys

Author Barry Kluczyk and the 1984 Mustang GT Turbo that served as the guinea pig for his engine rebuild project.

to success are planning, patience, and attention to detail.

If you invested in this book, you're probably like me—an enthusiast who is fairly comfortable under the hood, but has never attempted a complete engine removal/rebuild/reinstallation project. I'd worked on engines before writing this book and helped with a few engine swaps, but I'd never attempted the whole project solo.

It should be noted that while this book covers the general steps required to remove an engine, disassemble it, and then rebuild and reinstall it, it couldn't illustrate all of the steps required for every vehicle. There are simply too many vehicle-specific design features and removal/replacement procedures,

but wherever possible I have tried point out or use photos to illustrate differences in procedures for inline-style and V-style engines or front-wheel drive and rear-drive configurations.

Fortunately, the vast majority of steps and the cadence of them are similar, regardless of the vehicle's drive configuration or engine type. That said, the builder who attempts this project needs to arm himself or herself with either factory service manuals or the aftermarket repair guides from Haynes, Chilton, etc. They will provide additional guidance on vehicle-specific components, removal steps, and, most importantly, the torque and tolerance specifications required during the engine assembly stage.

As described in Chapter 1, you'll also need some tools and materials that aren't likely in your home garage. If you haven't got one, this project gives you a bona fide reason to buy a torque wrench. Like me, you may also wind up with a shiny-new shop crane in the corner of your shop, too. The accomplishment of the project proved that it was well within my grasp and I'm not afraid to break out that crane and use it again on the next wayward old car that winds up in my driveway.

I approached my rebuild project as a challenge, not a chore. I hope you will, too, and I hope this book helps to make your project a smooth, enjoyable, and satisfying experience.

WHAT IS A WORKBENCH® BOOK?

This Workbench® Series book is the only book of its kind on the market. No other book offers the same combination of detailed hands-on information and revealing color photographs to illustrate engine rebuilding. Rest assured, you have purchased an indispensable companion that will expertly guide you, one step at a time, through each important stage of the rebuilding process. This book is packed with real world techniques and practical tips for expertly performing rebuild procedures, not vague instructions or unnecessary processes. At-home mechanics or enthusiast builders strive for professional results, and the instruction in our Workbench® Series books help you realize pro-caliber results. Hundreds of photos guide you through the entire process from start to finish, with informative captions containing comprehensive instructions for every step of the process.

Appendixes located in the back of the book provide essential specification and rebuild information. These include diagrams and charts for cylinder firing order, torque sequences and specifications, piston ring gap alignment, and timing belt/chain alignment. In addition, general engine specifications, including compression ratio, bore and stroke, oil pressure, and many other specifications, are included.

The step-by-step photo procedures also contain many additional photos that show how to install high-performance components, modify stock components for special applications, or even call attention to assembly steps that are critical to proper operation or safety. These are labeled with unique icons. These symbols represent an idea, and photos marked with the icons contain important, specialized information.

Here are some of the icons found in Workbench® books:

 Important!— Calls special attention to a step or procedure, so that the procedure is correctly performed. This prevents damage to a vehicle, system, or component.

 Save Money— Illustrates a method or alternate method of performing a rebuild step that will save money but still give acceptable results.

 Torque Fasteners— Illustrates a fastener that must be properly tightened with a torque wrench at this point in the rebuild. The torque specs are usually provided in the step.

 Special Tool— Illustrates the use of a special tool that may be required or can make the job easier (caption with photo explains further).

Performance Tip— Indicates a procedure or modification that can improve performance. Step most often applies to high-performance or racing engines.

 Critical Inspection— Indicates that a component must be inspected to ensure proper operation of the engine.

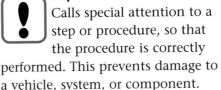 **Precision Measurement—** Illustrates a precision measurement or adjustment that is required at this point in the rebuild.

Professional Mechanic Tip— Illustrates a step in the rebuild that non-professionals may not know. It may illustrate a shortcut, or a trick to improve reliability, prevent component damage, etc.

Documentation Required— Illustrates a point in the rebuild where the reader should write down a particular measurement, size, part number, etc. for later reference or photograph a part, area or system of the vehicle for future reference.

 Tech Tip— Tech Tips provide brief coverage of important subject matter that doesn't naturally fall into the text or step-by-step procedures of a chapter. Tech Tips contain valuable hints, important info, or outstanding products that professionals have discovered after years of work. These will add to your understanding of the process, and help you get the most power, economy, and reliability from your engine.

PREPARATION AND TOOLS

The task of removing, rebuilding, and reinstalling the engine of a car, truck, or SUV is more accurately described as a series of interconnected sub-projects that all fall under the large umbrella of the primary project: getting the vehicle back on the road. Those sub-projects comprise the topics of each chapter in this book. Strategizing the work, materials, and expectations of the overall project is easier when tackled in this manner. The following chapters in this book illustrate the numerous tasks or sub-projects and show them in the approximate order in which they should be started and completed. This chapter focuses on the preparation, materials, and tools needed to get the project started.

Preparation is the key to a successful and time-efficient project. Although removing, rebuilding, and reinstalling an automotive engine is a project that can be tackled by those with limited mechanical skill or experience, the procedures involved require strategic thinking, contingency planning, and reconnaissance. It is no fun to discover that, with the car immobilized with a partially extracted engine, a tool is required that isn't in your toolbox. For those very reasons, you should do as much research as possible before starting the engine removal and acquire the tools, materials, and knowledge needed for the job. This means reading the factory service manual or an equivalent aftermarket repair manual prior to grabbing the first wrench.

Factory Service and Repair Manuals

Don't attempt this project without a set of factory service manuals and/or aftermarket repair manuals. Even if you are familiar with the underhood environment of your vehicle, you need the guidance provided by the manuals. In most cases,

The vehicle, the home shop (garage), and an enthusiast's ambition form the foundation for an engine-rebuild project. Before the toolbox and shop crane are pushed into place, research and prep work is necessary to ensure a straightforward, high-quality, and accurate process. It is a project that can even be accomplished by novice builders who have never previously removed an engine or rebuilt it.

they provide the basic steps for engine removal, as well as describe specialty tools or hardware involved with engine removal, engine teardown, and engine assembly. For example, if you are unsure whether the engine is removed from the top (up and out of the engine compartment) or from the bottom (lowered out of the chassis on a cradle), the manuals will provide this basic but vital information.

These manuals also provide the specifications to which the engine should be rebuilt, with charts on torque specifications, component usage, and other details. You will not want to start the engine assembly without a copy of these specifications.

Aftermarket repair manuals for more popular and later-model vehicles, commonly known by their publishers—such as those from Chilton, Hayes, and Clymer—are generally available at most auto parts stores. They're also available online through sites such as eBay.

Factory service manuals, particularly for older models, can be harder to find and are considerably more expensive. A complete set of manuals, which typically include electrical, chassis, and body sections, can be had for only a few dollars for some models and upward of $200 for others. Manuals for later-model cars can usually be ordered through a dealership parts department. They're also available online at sites such as www.autorepairmanuals.biz. Also, eBay is an excellent source for finding factory manuals. The publisher of this book, CarTech Books, also has an extensive library of model-specific how-to books that can be of additional assistance; the available titles can be found at www.cartechbooks.com.

But for all their reference assistance, service manuals are notoriously vague on some topics or procedures. It is all too common to encounter instructions that don't provide some of the nuanced details of the procedure or trouble-shooting

1984 Car Shop Manual

Powertrain Lubrication Maintenance

All Models Except Tempo/Topaz, Escort/Lynx, EXP

Ford

Factory service manuals provide necessary removal and installation steps, as well as important information on reconditioning specifications. Often, factory manuals explain essential techniques and procedures for an engine rebuild and are absolutely crucial for first-time builders. Even if the manuals cost $200 to $300, it's money well spent. A factory manual can save the first-time builder from making a fundamental mistake that could ruin the entire engine build-up.

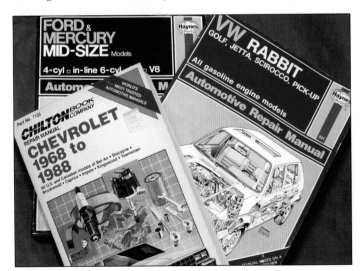

If a factory service manual cannot be obtained, an aftermarket repair manual from one of the major publishers, such as Haynes or Chilton, is an acceptable alternative, but these manuals typically don't offer the depth of information that is found in factory service manuals.

For the Ford engine shown throughout this book, we used a combination of the factory service manual and an aftermarket repair manual. Referencing both was helpful at different points during the project because they provided essential information for completing various procedures for the first-time or novice builder.

Cylinder	
Diameter	4.0000 to 4.0048 in
Taper limit	0.010 in
Out-of-round limit	0.005 in
Deck warpage limit	0.003 in per 6 in
Pistons and rings	
Piston diameter	
Coded red	3.9982 to 3.9998 in
Coded blue	3.9994 to 4.0000 in
Piston-to-cylinder bore clearance	0.0014 to 0.0022 in
Piston ring-to-groove clearance	
Top compression	0.0019 to 0.0036 in
Bottom compression	0.002 to 0.004 in
Oil	Snug fit in groove
Service limit	0.002 in max increase in
Piston ring end gap	
Top compression	0.010 to 0.020 in
Bottom compression	0.010 to 0.020 in
Oil (1975 and 1976)	0.015 to 0.055 in
Piston pin diameter (standard)	0.9749 to 0.9754 in
Piston pin-to-piston clearance	0.0003 to 0.0005 in
Piston pin-to-connecting rod bushing clearance	Interference fit
Crankshaft and flywheel	
Main journal	
Diameter	2.9994 to 3.0002 in
Taper limit — max per inch	0.0005 in
Out-of-rounnd limit	0.0006 in
Runout limit	
TIR maximum	0.002 in
Service limit	0.005 in
Main bearing oil clearance	
Desired	0.0008 to 0.0015 in
Allowable	0.0008 to 0.0026 in
Connecting rod journal	

Rebuild specifications for engine components are the most valuable pieces of information contained in service or repair manuals. This information is critical, and the builder should not attempt to assemble the engine without it.

suggestions. Still, it's difficult to overstate the importance of these manuals. Be sure to acquire a set prior to starting your project and read the pertinent sections before turning the first wrench.

Top-Out or Bottom-Out Removal

The first process to establish before starting the project is the method in which the vehicle's engine is removed and consequently reinstalled. There are two basic methods: top-out, or bottom-out. The top-out method is the most common and involves pulling the engine (with or without the transmission attached) up and out of the top of the engine compartment. Conversely, the bottom-out method is just as the term implies: the engine is lowered out of the engine compartment from the bottom of the vehicle. This is more common on later-model cars that have modular chassis engine-cradle assemblies or fast-rake windshields that extend

Extracting the engine through the top of the engine compartment is the most common method of engine removal, particularly for rear-drive vehicles. With the right tools, this removal method can be accomplished in a home garage.

Some vehicles demand a "bottom-out" engine removal that will likely require the use of a lift to separate the engine cradle from the chassis. This method may not be suitable for home garages that do not have the lifting equipment to raise the vehicle body high enough to safely pull the engine down and away from the chassis. If that is the case, the builder needs to seek professional assistance when removing and installing the engine.

over the engine compartment, making it difficult to pull the engine from the top.

Both methods have their advantages and challenges; the top-out method can be easier to accomplish in a home garage, while the bottom-out method generally reduces the amount of time required to disconnect ancillary components. Generally speaking, front-wheel-drive cars tend to have more bottom-out-type extraction and installation procedures, but there are numerous rear-drive examples, such as the 1993–2002 Chevy Camaro and Pontiac Firebird.

A service manual should provide the necessary information for the recommended removal method. If it's unclear, a quick check on websites devoted to the vehicle model can provide additional information or direction. Much of the remainder of preparation and the acquisition of tools depend on the extraction/installation method that you employ.

Workspace

Identify the workspace that you will use to remove the engine from the vehicle and, likely, reinstall it. A garage with a flat, concrete floor is optimal. If the space is in a two-car garage or larger, try to position the vehicle toward the center of the floor; this provides more room on either side of the vehicle for maneuvering and component extraction.

If it is your first attempt at a project of this magnitude and you are using mostly hand tools for the job, the vehicle will likely remain in its position for several days. After the engine is removed, the vehicle will be significantly lighter and therefore

easier to move. It can be pushed over to the side of a two-stall garage, freeing up the space for another car during the time of the engine's teardown and rebuilding stages. When it's time to reinstall the engine, position the car, again, at the center of the garage floor.

If the vehicle requires a bottom-out removal process, a lift may be required. If that is the case, you may need to seek professional assistance with the engine's removal.

Lighting

It seems an obvious detail to mention, as every garage has lighting, but a couple of overhead bulbs or even a couple of ceiling-mounted fluorescent lights are inadequate for

the procedures outlined in this book, whether during the engine removal stage or engine assembly.

Easily obtainable and affordable halogen work lamps are excellent for the job. A stand-mounted twin-head lamp is great for flooding a garage or work area with bright, even light. This is particularly important during the engine teardown and assembly stages, in which precision and attention to detail are critically important.

Bench-type halogen work lights are very helpful, too, as they can be positioned beneath the vehicle or aimed under the hood. Additionally, fluorescent-type "trouble" lights with magnetic bases and handheld flashlights will all come in handy for the project. LED-type flashlights provide

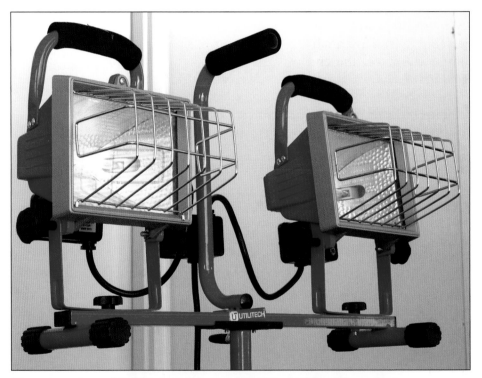

The value of good lighting can't be underestimated for this project. Adjustable-head halogen work lamps provide exceptional light for under-lit home garages. These lamps are available from almost every home improvement store, hardware store, and large retail outlets such as Kmart, Sears, etc. Prices range from only a few dollars to more than $100 for professional-grade lamps. A floor lamp with a tall, adjustable stand is preferred.

excellent light in dark recesses of an engine compartment, making it easier to locate bolts and hardware.

Digital Camera

While not usually found in a toolbox, a camera for recording the stages of engine removal and engine teardown is a wise idea for novice builders. Simply put, there are many, many connections, unique component orientations, and specific hose/line routings, and you will not remember them all when it comes time to reassemble the engine and reinstall it in the vehicle. Shooting reference photos will prove invaluable when it comes to double-checking the cadence and sequence of assembly and installation procedures.

Yes, pausing to take photos with every few steps adds time to the project, but it is an essential "tool" that ultimately makes the end processes go quicker.

Gloves and Hand Cleaner

Another rather obvious detail, but the point here isn't to simply suggest work gloves and hand cleaner, it's to warn that you should stock up on them because you won't believe how much you'll need them. And if the engine project is something you're doing in addition to a regular home and work routine, the cleaner you keep your hands, the more you will appreciate it.

Investing in a set of quality gloves, such as those from Mechanix Wear, is wise because these gloves provide excellent dexterity for most projects. They can cost $20 to $40 a pair, but are well worth it. Be warned, though, these gloves keep most dirt and grime off the hands, but because they're breathable, they don't prevent oil from soaking through to the skin.

A box of medical-style latex gloves is another excellent method for keeping hands cleaner during the project. They're cheap, disposable, and can be worn under Mechanix Gloves for a double layer of protection.

When it comes to hand cleaners, any of the popular types, whether the petroleum-based cleaners such as GOJO, or abrasive types such as Fast Orange, will do the trick; just make sure you have plenty on hand. You'll go through lots of it, so don't underestimate your needs. Buy the big bottle.

Along the same lines, have plenty of rags at the ready. You'll use all of them and more, so build up your inventory before starting the project.

Oil Dry

Go to the auto parts store and load up with several bags of oil dry and/or kitty litter. Even the best laid plans for avoiding fluid spills will go awry, and it is inevitable that oil, coolant, transmission fluid, and more will spill out onto your garage floor. Plan for it and keep an open bag of oil dry at the ready.

Engine Lift/Shop Crane

Although many vehicles are designed for bottom-type engine removal, where the engine is lowered out of the chassis, most vehicles have a top-out procedure, whereby the engine is pulled up and out through the top of the engine compartment. And if you've got a vintage, air-cooled Volkswagen Beetle, give the engine a bear hug and remember to lift with the legs!

For the top-out method, an engine lifting mechanism, also called a shop crane, will be necessary. They are typically available in one- and two-ton capacities. A one-ton crane is sufficient for most 4-, 6-, and some 8-cylinder engines. However, projects involving heavier 8-cylinder engines, particularly those with a transmission to be removed simultaneously, are better off with a two-ton crane.

Another consideration of the shop crane is the reach of its boom.

Engine removal and disassembly is going to cause oil to spill. Drain pans and oil drying and/or absorbing materials should be at the ready as soon as the project begins.

The adjustable load leveler adjusts the balance of the engine during removal or installation. This is particularly helpful when extracting an engine, with the transmission attached, from a rear-drive vehicle. With the leveler, the weight balance of the assembly can be manually adjusted during extraction, shifting the weight bias as needed to a more balanced position. The engine or engine/transmission assembly can be removed on a more stable and level plane, making for a safer procedure. It also helps reduce the tendency for fluid leaks and inadvertent contact of the engine with the vehicle body.

Shop cranes with foldable legs are available, making them very easy to store even in small garages. If the builder is considering purchasing a crane for his or her home shop, a unit with fold-up legs is absolutely the one to select.

A shop crane (also called an engine hoist) is needed to pull an engine up and out of a vehicle. For those who don't plan to perform such projects very often, renting will suffice. However, shop cranes have become increasingly affordable, and the investment in one will pay for itself after two or three projects.
A higher-capacity crane is recommended, even if the capacity seems much greater than the estimated weight of the engine, because a higher-capacity crane is typically large and has a longer boom. This provides greater leverage and maneuverability, particularly on vehicles that are taller or have longer front-end sheet metal.

Generally, a one-ton crane has a shorter boom than a two-ton crane, so vehicles that have a longer front end, such as rear-drive vehicles, may benefit from the security offered by a one-ton crane, even if the engine is a lighter-weight 4- or 6-cylinder.

And no, this is not a tool most casual enthusiasts have stashed in their garage, and many at-home enthusiasts get stalled on starting their project because of this detail. There are a few options that make this an easily jumped hurdle:

Rent it. In most areas, these cranes are easily obtained through rental companies—the same companies that rent tools, trailers, etc. Some companies will even deliver the crane. The daily rental fee is typically low, but the key to success is anticipating when you'll need it. Don't reserve the crane *before* you've started disassembling the ancillary items around the engine, such as the cooling system, transmission, etc. Invariably, you'll encounter unforeseen hang-ups with these procedures and a day's or weekend's rental could be wasted because you weren't quite ready to use the crane. Wait until *after* the ancillary items are out of the way before scheduling the crane rental, even if it means waiting an extra day or two. In the long run, you'll be time and money ahead of the game. And don't forget, you'll have to rent the crane again for the engine's installation.

Buy it. For most enthusiasts, this doesn't sound like a viable option, mostly because of the cost involved and space required to store such a large item. However, the proliferation in recent years of inexpensive, typically Chinese-manufactured tools has drastically reduced the cost of what used to be professional-only tools. Also, many shop cranes are available with foldable legs that enable them to be stored in relatively little space. Stores such as Harbor Freight are among the largest purveyors of these inexpensive, "offshore" tools.

Some professionals and enthusiasts contend that seemingly cut-rate tools lack sufficient quality. And while they may not be the types of tools that are found in, say, a NASCAR team's garage, they are generally excellent, low-cost options for at-home enthusiasts. In fact, for this book I purchased an inexpensive, folding shop crane. It has proved sturdy, durable, and has given no reason to suggest otherwise.

Tow it. For those who don't have the local means for rental or the capacity to purchase a shop crane, the last resort is professional pulling. You can still enjoy the satisfaction of rebuilding an engine yourself, even if you take the vehicle to a professional shop to have the engine removed. A way to reduce the cost of the removal and increase the level of personal involvement on the project is to remove as much of the ancillary components as possible—the less the shop has to do, the less it will cost you. For example, you can drain the cooling system, remove the radiator, drain other engine fluids, and even remove the transmission. The professional shop will be left with little more than pulling out the core engine. Of course, this requires having the vehicle transported to and from the shop, but if getting a shop crane to your home garage is out of the question, this is the best alternative.

Jacks and Jack Stands

Hydraulic floor jacks and jack stands are a must for the project. In some cases, more than one floor jack will be required. Generally, the jacks and jack stands will be used to raise the car during the stages of engine removal and installation that involve the transmission, exhaust system, and other underbody components.

For some vehicles, the transmission will be disconnected from the engine and removed prior to the engine's removal. In these cases, the jack stands need to be tall enough to

provide enough underbody clearance to lower the transmission—usually while it is strapped to a floor jack—and pull it out from beneath the vehicle. Generally, this is approximately 18 inches (46 cm) or a little less. As mentioned above, transmission removal will likely involve the use of a typical hydraulic floor jack, and, in some cases, a pair of them makes the job easier to accomplish.

Jack stands will likely be used to support underbody components, such as the transmission or exhaust system, so it may be necessary to have six to eight jack stands on hand—four to support the vehicle, and the others for underbody uses. Be aware that most jack stands will not provide enough clearance under the vehicle for a bottom-out-type engine removal. Additional lift supports or an alternate method of extraction will likely be required.

Vehicle Lifts

More and more enthusiasts have installed drive-on hydraulic vehicle lifts in their home garage. This can enhance and speed the process of some tasks, such as transmission removal in most cars, which also allows for the use of a specialized transmission jack stand, but it also presents some challenges.

Many home-type vehicle lifts have no provision for jacking up the front wheels, which may require removal for access to certain components, particularly in front-wheel-drive vehicles. The drive-on-style lifts, which are designed more for creating two-level storage in a single-story garage, also can inhibit exhaust removal.

Finally, the very design of drive-on lifts makes it impossible to perform bottom-out engine removal or

In addition to the standard floor jack, a set of four jack stands should be used to support the car during the engine removal stage. As with the shop crane, the highest-capacity stands should be used to ensure safety.

installation, because the engine is typically lowered onto a factory cradle that also includes the front axles. With the vehicle's front end resting on the lift ramps, it's impossible to lower the engine/axle cradle assembly.

Engine Stand

For the at-home rebuild project, a permanent investment in an engine stand is recommended. It is an item not typically rented, but they are relatively inexpensive. They are generally priced by their size and capacity, with the most common stands rated between 1,000 and 1,500 pounds. This is sufficient for most engines, although some older Detroit iron, such as big-block engines with cast-iron intake manifolds and heavy exhaust manifolds, will push the limit of these stands. Most stands accommodate inline and V-style engines. Air-cooled auto engines, such as those from Volkswagen or Porsche, typically require an adapter or a dedicated stand designed specifically for them. The same goes for some flat or "pancake" engines.

Engine Stand Bolt Hardware

When it comes time to mount the engine on an engine stand, you will need approximately four to eight bolts that secure the stand's attachment bracket to the engine block; they are not included with the engine stand. The bolts need to be at least a quarter of an inch to half an inch longer than the attachment bracket "fingers," in order to provide enough "bite" to hold the engine securely. The bolts are threaded into the holes that otherwise secure the automatic transmission or manual transmission bellhousing. Determining the size and length of the bracket bolts is achieved by measuring the length of the bracket fingers and adding at least a quarter-inch; and knowing the bolt size of the transmission/bellhousing bolts (3/8 inch,

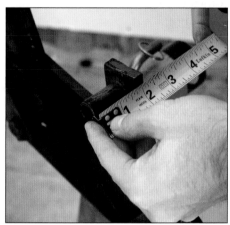

The correct length for the engine attachment hardware must be determined because it's not included with the engine stand. It involves measuring the attachment "fingers" on the stand's head.

An engine stand is not typically rented, so it must be purchased for the project. A 1,500-pound capacity stand should be sufficient for most engines, while adapters may be required for some unconventional engines, such as "pancake" and air-cooled engines. Most V-8 engines weigh between 500 to 800 lbs while certain diesel engines and other larger engines can weight in excess of 1,000 lbs. Even seemingly lightweight four-cylinder engines can be heavier than expected, especially if they use a cast-iron cylinder block.

The bolts to hold the engine to the stand should be a quarter-inch to a half-inch longer than the stand's fingers. Large washers are usually also needed for security because the engine is typically attached through the bellhousing bolt holes. The removal of one of those bolts will determine the correct size and thread style.

12 mm, etc). The removal of a single transmission or bellhousing bolt prior to the project's start provides an example of the correct bolt size. Taking care of this seemingly minor detail before the engine disassembly procedure begins can save much time and aggravation when it comes time to mount the engine on the stand.

A breaker bar is a necessary tool that is used for breaking loose main cap bolts, head bolts, and other stubborn bolts, such as those on the exhaust manifold. It is also used to turn the rotating assembly after the pistons have been installed.

Hand Tools and Impact Tools

A variety of hand tools are required during all of the different stages of the project. Some are not needed during the removal stage, so it is not necessary, for example, to have a torque wrench ready when disconnecting the transmission. A list of the tools generally needed for the various aspects of the project is included in this chapter, but a few words about hand tools versus the use of air-powered impact tools is warranted.

Air tools can be a tremendous aid during the removal and installation stages of the project because they speed fastening and unfastening of hardware, but you must be careful not to over torque or strip fasteners. Some engine builders will also use air tools for some aspects of engine teardown or assembly. Since it is easy to make a costly mistake and overtorque a fastener, it's not a good idea for most novice builders to use air tools for many delicate engine disassembly and assembly procedures.

If you do not have much experience disassembling and rebuilding an engine, use only hand tools when it comes to the engine itself. Air tools are fine for removing the transmission or exhaust system, but attention to detail with the engine components is so very critical. The slower pace of hand tools will enhance focus and provide for a more complete understanding of the feel of components and their relationships with one another.

Beyond the basic wrench and socket set, you need deep-well sockets, swivel-head attachments, and, most important of all, a breaker bar with a half-inch drive. The breaker bar is needed for loosening head bolts, main cap bolts, and turning the engine's rotating assembly. It is an essential tool for the rebuild process. Also, the socket size required to grasp the crankshaft hub or balancer bolt when rotating the engine is typically quite large, such as 20 mm, 22 mm, or greater; it may not be part of most basic socket sets. You will likely have to invest in these large-size sockets.

Beyond the typical socket set, the project requires deep-well sockets and large-diameter sockets. Half-inch-drive sockets and ratchets are usually required for main bearing caps and cylinder head bolts because they will be used with a torque wrench.

Torque Wrenches and Angle Meters

Another investment for the project, if it isn't already in your toolbox,

The torque wrench is a basic tool of the engine assembly process. They can be very expensive, but moderately priced examples are easy to find and deliver excellent results. Many professionals use Mac and Snap-on torque wrenches, but there other excellent wrenches suitable for the at-home builder from manufacturers such as Sears, Craftsman, and Kobalt. For those who will use a torque wrench only occasionally, he or she should plan to spend about $100 for a torque wrench.

Conventional torque wrenches are equipped with foot-pound and Newton-meter settings, which may not be suitable for some later-model engines that use torque-to-yield fasteners. These engines require a wrench that torques to a maximum angle after a minimum torque spec is achieved.

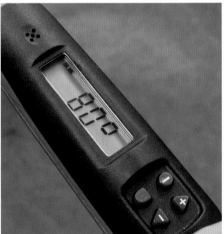

A torque wrench with an angle meter or degree setting is needed for torque-to-yield fasteners. This Snap-on electronic wrench can be programmed for foot-pounds, Newton meters, and torque angle degrees. Non-electronic angle meters typically use a fan-shaped dial and pointer that the builder uses as a guide for the final torque procedure.

is a torque wrench. The engine assembly simply cannot take place without it. Torque wrenches vary greatly in price, but a moderate-to-midlevel-priced wrench should suffice. The traditional torque wrench works by setting the gauge or meter to a specific torque limit, in foot-pounds or Newton-meters. The wrench provides an audible sound and "click" feel when torque limit is achieved. However, many late-model engines now use "torque-to-yield" fasteners that, after being torqued to a preliminary torque setting, are final-torqued to a specific degree from the lower setting. For example, the water pump on a GM LS V-8 engine is typically final-torqued to 18 degrees past the preliminary torque setting.

Conventional torque wrenches are not equipped for torque-to-yield settings, so if you have an engine with these fasteners, a torque angle meter is required. Some pricier, electronic-readout torque wrenches offer both traditional torque settings and torque angle settings, but it is likely you will have to acquire a torque angle meter to complement the torque wrench.

Engine-Building Tools and Materials

Beyond the general hand tools and specialty tools, there are a number of specific tools and materials required during the engine removal and assembly that, if you have never attempted such a project, are probably not in your toolbox. Depending on the engine and application, these tools and materials can include:

Dial indicator tool: used for checking crankshaft endplay and other tolerances; this may be rented or substituted in many cases with a feeler gauge.

Distributor wrench: needed on some engines with difficult-to-access distributors, particularly V-8 engines with rear-mounted distributors.

Engine assembly lube: required on many moving components during the assembly stage.

Engine-specific tools: additionally, there are tools with specific applications used only on a single engine type; for example, a timing-chain installation tool for a specific engine family, such as Ford modular V-8 engines or Nissan inline-4 engines. Also, some

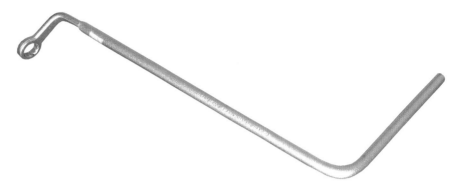

A tailshaft plug is needed when removing a transmission with the engine. They are not typically found at auto parts stores, so you may need to search catalogs or online sources for one. We purchased this one at an automotive swap meet.

Not required for all engines, but a distributor wrench comes in very handy for hard-to-reach distributors, such as the rear-mounted distributors on Chevy small-block and big-block engines. It is a relatively inexpensive tool that can greatly ease removal and installation of the distributor.

Motor oil is not sufficient for lubrication for every component and system on an automotive engine. Assembly lube is a must when it's time to build the engine; it is available at almost every auto parts outlet. Assembly lube is applied to a wide variety of components throughout the assembly process, including cams, lifter faces, and rod bearings.

There are numerous types of piston ring compressors, but the universal, adjustable compressor, such as the one seen here, is suitable for the amateur builder. This one was found in the tool department at Sears. Other types of compressors are sized to the specific bore diameter, such as 3.500 inches or, in the case of a 0.030-inch overbore, 3.530 inches. These custom-sized compressors are generally more expensive than universal compressors.

engines may require a unique tool for specific procedures, such as relieving fuel pressure. Such requirements underscore the need for you to scan the service manual prior to beginning the project, so that all the necessary tools are on hand when they're needed.

Feeler gauge: used to check a variety of tolerances during the assembly stage.

Oil priming tool: some engines require a special tool to help prime the oiling system prior to starting the engine for the first time. The service manual should provide guidance on whether it is required for a specific engine.

Piston ring compressor: used to squeeze the rings against the piston in order to slip the piston into the cylinder.

Plastigage: a "soft" tool used for checking bearing tolerances.

Pulley puller: necessary on some engines to remove and install

crankshaft dampers, balancers, and/or pulleys; pullers vary, so you should check the service manual to see which style is required.

Timing light: when the engine is started for the first time, it requires ignition-timing adjustments that are checked and confirmed with a timing light. This doesn't apply to engines with a distributorless ignition system.

Transmission tailshaft plug: prevents fluid leaking when the transmission is disconnected and removed.

Tools and Materials List

Engine Removal
Wrenches, sockets, and
    screwdrivers
Floor jack
Jack stands (4)
Drain pan(s)
Shop crane
Transmission tailshaft plug
Pry bar
Engine stand
Oil dry
Misc. bolts and nuts (for lift chain)

Engine Disassembly
Shop crane
Engine stand
Sockets, including deep-wells
Wrenches
Screwdrivers/nut drivers
Timing belt/chain removal tool
    (overhead-cam engines)
Breaker bar
Pulley puller
Penetrating oil
Gasket scraper

Short-Block Assembly
Engine stand
Torque wrench and/or torque
    angle meter
Sockets, including deep-wells
Wrenches
Screwdrivers/nut drivers
Feeler gauge and/or dial-indicator
    instrument
Piston ring compressor/piston
    installation tool
Engine assembly lube
Camshaft/lifter lube (if required)
RTV-type (or equivalent) sealer
Thread sealant
Plastigage

Engine Final Assembly
Torque wrench and/or torque
    angle meter

An oil-priming tool is required for some engines, mostly V-6 and V-8 engines that use the distributor to drive the oil pump. This tool should be used whenever possible, because it greatly reduces the chance for non-lubricated friction between parts at start-up. Engines that don't use a distributor to turn the oil pump must rely on alternate methods of oil priming, such as a complicated vacuum procedure or a non-fueled or no-spark "rollover" procedure that spins the engine without starting in order to circulate the engine oil. These procedures will work on engines with a distributor-driven oil pump, but the priming method and tool described here makes the task much easier.

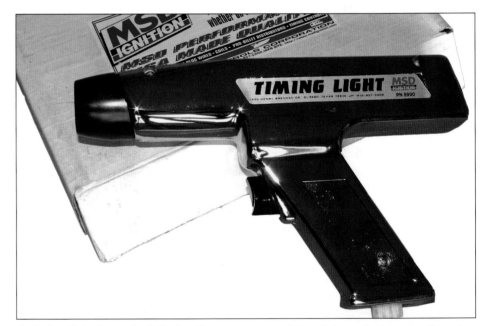

A timing light is needed during the start-up and break-in period to check and set ignition timing for engines that use a conventional distributor. It easily clips to the vehicle's ignition system to verify and, as needed, confirm adjustments to the timing on the number-1 cylinder. Later-model engines that do not have a distributor do not require the use of a timing light because timing adjustments are typically made automatically by a computer-controlled ignition system.

Sockets, including deep-wells	Engine assembly lube
Breaker bar	RTV-type
Wrenches	(or equivalent) sealer
Screwdrivers/nut drivers	Thread sealant

Engine Installation
Shop crane
Floor jack
Oil dry
Sockets, including deep-wells
Wrenches
Screwdrivers/nut drivers

Start-Up, Tuning and Break-In
Oil
Coolant
Oil priming tool
Timing light

The Engine Shown Throughout this Book

Many types and brands of engines are seen in the photos of this book, but the primary engine that is the focus of the removal, rebuilding, and reinstallation project is a 2.3-liter turbocharged 4-cylinder overhead-cam engine from a 1984 Ford Mustang GT Turbo.

When it was introduced in the 1983 model year, the fuel-injected and turbocharged 2.3-liter engine was an early example of modern engine design that would become standard in most passenger vehicles. It used a computer-controlled, port-fuel-injection system that was rare for its day but the same basic air-fuel configuration. Virtually all cars use this type of engine-control system today. Yet, for its advanced air-fuel control, the engine still used a conventional distributor-type ignition system and V-belt-type engine-driven accessories rather than a crank-fired ignition and serpentine belt system. In short, it is an engine configured like most modern examples, but with holdover details from a previous era. As such, it is an excellent example of the type of engine

rebuild project that is encountered everyday by builders everywhere.

The engine was disassembled in a home garage that was equipped with few specialty tools and no air compressor; no impact tools were used during the project. The cylinder block, head, and other components were sent to a machine shop for refurbishment. The turbocharger was sent via a shipping service to a rebuilding service that installed new seals, reconditioned the housing, and return-shipped it. The engine was assembled and re-installed at home. A shop crane and other necessary tools were purchased for the project.

A majority of the photos in the chapters on tear-down, short-block assembly, final assembly, and engine installation depict the Ford engine, but wherever possible, I (as author/builder) have augmented the depiction of the overhead-cam 4-cylinder with photos and descriptions of pushrod (cam-in-block) V-type engines and other engines.

The engine and the car belong to me. The car is a relatively rare model and its engine refurbishment was part of a budget restoration that also included bodywork, paint, and interior restoration. Only 3,241 GT Turbo models were sold in 1984 and only 654 of them were black, like mine.

Common Terms

Auxiliary shaft: Typically found on overhead-cam and/or inline-type engines, this camshaft-like device is crankshaft driven and used to drive engine components, such as the distributor or oil pump.

Bearing clearance: The space between a component (such as the crankshaft or camshaft) and the bearing that is occupied by a film of oil.

Boring or over-boring: The machining process in which a cutting tool slightly enlarges a cylinder bore in order to make it comply with factory specifications for roundness and finish.

Cam-in-block engine: An engine that has its camshaft located inside the cylinder block and the pushrod-actuated valves located above it; also called a pushrod engine or overhead-valve engine.

Cast: Manufacturing method in which components, usually associated with pistons, are formed with liquefied metal that is poured into a mold.

Coil-near-plug or coil-on-plug: Individual ignition coils that are mounted directly above or near their corresponding spark plugs; used with distributorless ignition systems.

Crate engine: A pre-built engine assembly generally consisting of a long block or more that is generally ready for installation; so-named for the wooden crate container in which most are delivered.

Crosshatch pattern: The finish texture on cylinder bores that is necessary to retain oil and provide a seating surface for the piston rings.

Damper: An anti-vibration device, also called a balancer, which is mounted to the front of the crankshaft and may or may not include the crankshaft drive pulley.

Decking: The machining process whereby a small amount of material is ground off the cylinder deck of an engine block in order to make it perfectly flat.

Distributorless ignition: Found on many late-model engines, this ignition system does not use a conventional, engine-driven distributor; rather, toothed wheels on the crankshaft and camshaft are "read" by sensors to synchronize ignition timing.

Fuel rail: The assembly on a port-fuel-injected engine that holds the injectors and delivers fuel to them.

Forged: Construction method typically associated with pistons and crankshafts in which metal is "pounded" or formed into the desired shape; widely considered to be stronger than cast parts.

Hone or honing: The process of giving the cylinder bore its final finish, including the crosshatch pattern.

Hydraulic camshaft/valvetrain: Camshaft configuration that uses lifters with hydraulic chambers to reduce friction and eliminate the need for valve lash maintenance adjustments.

Hypereutectic: An alloy used in the construction of cast aluminum pistons.

Inline engine: An engine with all the cylinders located in a single bank above the crankshaft.

Long block: A partial engine assembly including a complete reciprocating assembly, oil pan, oil pump, etc., and including the assembled and installed cylinder heads.

Magnaflux: Brand name of a crack-inspection method that uses iron particles and a magnet.

OE/OEM: Abbreviation for Original Equipment or Original Equipment Manufacturer; a reference to the vehicle's builder, such as Ford, Toyota, or Volkswagen.

Overhead-cam engine (OHC): An engine that has the camshaft(s) located above the valves.

Overhead-valve engine: An engine that has its camshaft located inside the cylinder block and the pushrod-actuated valves located above it; also called cam-in-block or pushrod engine.

Piston-to-valve clearance: The space between the tallest part of the piston at the top of its stroke and the lowest part of a valve when it is open. Machining of the cylinder block and/or cylinder heads can reduce the clearance, possibly causing an interference problem.

Plastigage: Trade name for a crushable plastic tool that is used to determine bearing clearance.

Preload: The setup relationship of the pushrod between the lifter and the rocker arm.

Priming: The act of pressurizing the engine's oil system prior to start-up.

Port fuel injection: Fuel-injection system in which fuel is sprayed directly into the cylinder head intake ports, rather than first being mixed with air in a throttle body.

Pushrod engine: Vernacular term for a cam-in-block engine, named for the fact the valves are actuated by pushrods. See "Cam-in-block engine" and "Overhead-valve engine."

Remanufactured engine or "reman": A professionally rebuilt engine that is assembled to production specifications and designed as a direct replacement for a vehicle's original engine.

Roller lifters or "roller engine": An engine that uses lifters with rollers on the camshaft-side tips to reduce friction.

Roll-over: The act of "starting" the engine without fuel or ignition in order to prime the oil system.

Rotating assembly: The interconnected assembly of the crankshaft, connecting rods, and pistons.

Serpentine belt: A flat, long drive belt found on most later-model engines that typically transmits power to almost all of the engine's accessories.

Short block: A partial engine assembly including a complete reciprocating assembly, oil pan, oil pump, etc., but not including the cylinder heads.

Surfacing: The machining process whereby material is cut from the deck-mating surface of a cylinder head in order to make it absolutely flat.

Tappet: Another word for lifter.

Throttle body fuel injection (TBI): Fuel-injection system in which air and fuel are mixed before being drawn through the intake manifold and into the cylinder head intake ports. A carburetor-style injection unit characterizes this type of injection system.

Throttle body (port fuel injection): On a port-fuel-injection engine, the throttle body is the air inlet control component.

Torque-to-yield fastener: A non-reusable bolt that stretches to its final torque specification and requires a torque angle meter to achieve that final spec.

Valve lash: The relationship between the rocker arms, pushrod, and lifters on a cam-in-block engine with a flat-tappet camshaft.

V-belt: An older style of engine drive belt that is named for the thick, V-shape of the belt.

V-engine: An engine with opposing banks of cylinders and the pistons of those opposing cylinders connecting by a centrally located crankshaft.

ENGINE REMOVAL

Tools and Materials Required

- Wrenches, sockets and screwdrivers
- Floor jack
- Jack stands (4)
- Drain pan(s)
- Shop crane
- Transmission tailshaft plug
- Pry bar
- Engine stand
- Oil dry
- Misc. bolts and nuts (for lift chain)

Engine removal begins with the preparation of the vehicle. It should be located on a level surface that provides adequate room for sliding under the vehicle to disconnect and remove components and using a shop crane over the engine.

Of course, the battery should be disconnected before the first wrench is turned. In fact, some may find more room to maneuver under the hood if the battery is altogether removed.

The car should also be raised several inches and located on jack stands. This provides adequate space to slide under the vehicle—this goes for both rear-wheel-drive and front-wheel-drive vehicles. Front and rear jack stands should be used to keep the car level, reducing the likelihood of fluids pouring out during various stages of the engine removal.

A typical engine compartment of a front-drive car shows numerous components, such as the air cleaner assembly, a chassis support brace, and more items that also require removal in order to pull the transmission simultaneously with the engine. In this case, it is recommended that the engine be pulled independently of the transmission. In fact, the transmission need only be removed, in this case, if service is required.

Transmission Decision

The decision must be made whether to remove the combined transmission/engine assembly, remove the transmission separately, or to leave it in place. The service manual should be consulted for this aspect of the procedure because it can explain the easiest method. Most of the photos in this chapter show a conjoined engine/transmission extraction on a rear-wheel-drive vehicle.

When it comes to transverse-mounted (east-west mounted) front-drive vehicles, it may seem easy to simply unhook the engine from the transmission and pull only the engine, but that is not always the case. Hard-to-reach bellhousing bolts and other impediments may make the joint engine/transmission extraction ultimately an easier option.

Should the Hood Stay?

Adequate lifting space for engine extraction often comes down to whether the vehicle's hood is in the way. Many professionals will remove the hood during an engine removal, but it can be an awkward or almost impossible to do at home without the assistance of another person.

Cars and trucks built from at least the late 1980s typically have hoods that are supported by either a prop rod or hydraulic lift struts. With these vehicles, the hood can usually be opened to a completely vertical position, which offers plenty of room for extraction. Hoods with hydraulic struts require the struts' disconnection from the body.

Other vehicles, mostly mid- and full-size GM and Chrysler cars and trucks built from the 1950s through late 1980s, employ large, cumbersome hinge systems that do not allow the hood to open far enough for easy engine removal. This is also true of most late-model GM trucks and SUVs. With these vehicles, hood removal is the way to go.

Prior to unbolting the hood, however, the position of the hinge

Most of the procedural photos in this chapter show this 2.3-liter Ford four-cylinder engine, which is backed by a five-speed manual transmission. Given the age of the vehicle and an unknown repair history of the transmission, the transmission will be removed so that it can be inspected and possibly overhauled. Therefore, the engine and transmission will be removed as a single-assembly unit. However, this is not the only determining factor that should be considered when deciding to remove the transmission with the engine. In some cases, access to the fasteners that connect the engine and the transmission is prohibitively difficult, making it easier in the long run to remove the transmission with the engine.

The spring-loaded hood hinges of many domestic vehicles built through the late 1980s don't provide enough clearance to remove the engine. Therefore, the hoods on these vehicles must be removed. Two people are often required for such a job, as these hoods are typically very heavy and awkward to handle. A blanket, cardboard, or other protective item should be placed on the windshield during removal to prevent damage in case the hood inadvertently slips backward. Also, the position of the hinge bracket against the hood should be scribed onto the hood bottom prior to loosening the hinge bolts so that re-installation of the hood is more accurate.

On vehicles that have hydraulic struts to hold up the hood, the struts can be disconnected where they attach to the body. Usually, the struts can be simply "popped" off the mounts, so the hood can be raised nearly vertical, providing unimpeded space during the engine's extraction. A broomstick or other large rod can be used to hold the hood in the vertical position.

against the hood should be marked or scribed so that lining up the hood at the end of the project is easy and accurate.

Bottoms Up

While most car and truck engines can be removed by lifting them out of the top of the engine compartment, many vehicles built in the 1990s and later are designed to have the engine *lowered* out of the chassis. In many cases, this is ultimately an easier procedure, as the engine is typically mounted to an easily removable cradle or cross member. Again, check the service manual for the recommended procedure.

The "bottom-out" removal method cancels the need for a shop crane, but can cause challenges for the at-home builder. This is due to the vertical space required to move

GM's 1993–2002 Camaro and Firebird models are among the numerous vehicles in which engine removal involves a "bottom-out" extraction. The basic steps are shown in the next several photos, and the removal was performed at a professional shop, where a two-post lift was used to raise the body above the disconnected powertrain assembly.

the engine out and away from the body, approximately 36 inches.

If the engine is lowered out of the car, an adequate support system must be used to receive the engine cradle assembly, which often includes the transmission, front axles, suspension components, and sometimes the wheels. Most professional shops use a two-post lift to raise the body off the disconnected cradle, leaving the engine assembly on the floor.

Since most enthusiasts don't have a two-post lift in their garage, the alternative is raising the body high enough to provide sufficient room to move the engine and cradle assembly away from the body. Most jack stands won't provide the necessary clearance.

Options, then, are limited. Bypassing the factory recommendation and removing the engine from the top is possible for many vehicles, although the removal time may take longer. A careful inspection of the underhood area should be made before attempting this because some vehicles—

The bottom-out method starts with the disconnection of the front suspension and subframe from the chassis. This includes unbolting the shocks and control arms. There is generally no need to remove the shocks and/or coil springs because all of these components should remain assembled on the subframe.

With the suspension disconnected, the body is initially separated from the subframe, so the front wheels "fall" inward. At this point, the body is only raised a few inches so you can check for clearance and ensure all the necessary components are disconnected. Note that this shop placed the subframe on jack stands for the removal, giving the technicians more room to maneuver under the car. The process can be accomplished, too, by lifting the body with the wheels on the ground.

1993–2002 Camaros and Firebirds being prime examples—have "fast" windshield angles and/or cowls that extend over the engine, making top-out removal all but impossible.

With the body raised a few inches, a final check is made of the underbody components to make sure nothing will "hang up" on the chassis as it is raised farther. Proceeding slowly and methodically is the best way to ensure against damage.

The body is clearly free of the engine and subframe. The body doesn't need to be raised much farther. It needs to be raised high enough to make sure all of the subframe components are free and clear of the body, and to provide adequate room for the technicians to get at the engine.

Here's the completely separated engine and subframe. A closer look at the Camaro/Firebird powertrain shows the disconnected engine cradle, which includes the steering rack, brakes, axle spindles, and more. It may seem more complicated than simply pulling only the engine out through the top of the engine compartment, but there are fewer fasteners to disconnect with this method, making the bottom-out procedure relatively painless. However, the builder needs adequate room to drop the engine and move it away from the body. From here, the engine will be removed from the subframe, and the tear-down process will begin.

The home builder should make every attempt to gauge the removal space available in his or her garage because a disconnected cradle that still requires six more inches of vertical clearance space will very quickly ruin a good day's work on the project. In the end, professional assistance may be required to extract a bottom-out engine assembly.

General Removal Procedure

To ensure a time-effective and accurate removal process, I recommend working from front-to-back and top-to-bottom as a general method, meaning you should start at the front of the engine compartment and work rearward while simultaneously working from the top of the engine and moving downward. What follows in the accompanying photos and captions are the general removal steps for a rear-drive vehicle in which the engine and transmission are removed simultaneously, and through the top of the engine compartment. Most of the steps are similar for front-drive vehicles, while

1 Relieve Fuel Pressure

On some fuel-injected engines, it is necessary to relieve the pressure in the fuel line. This prevents the pressurized fuel from spraying the engine compartment when the fuel line is removed. For most vehicles, the procedure involves disconnecting an underhood relay and/or fuse and starting the engine, running it until the fuel flow ceases. The service manual should be consulted to determine whether this step is required. Other methods include disconnecting the fuel supply line or, depending on the vehicle, the access points on the fuel rail or pressure regulator. However, the vehicle's power must be disconnected in order to prevent surging from the fuel pump. The service manual should provide direction for the preferred relief method.

vehicles requiring a bottom-out extraction will have specific procedures that should be referenced from the manufacturer's service manual.

When relieving the engine's fuel pressure, the vehicle's gas cap should also be removed because minimal pressure in the tank can be enough to push fuel through the lines and cause it to spray in the engine compartment.

2 Disconnect Battery

Safety Step

 The negative battery cable should be removed from its post. In some vehicles, it is helpful to remove the battery, too, to create more workspace under the hood. If the battery is removed, it should be placed on a piece of wood to prevent unintended discharge.

3 Raise Vehicle and Install Jack Stands

The vehicle should be raised and placed on jack stands so that the vehicle is level. The vehicle should be high enough to afford easy access to underbody components, such as the transmission. Most vehicles have dedicated locations on the underbody for jacking, and the stands should be positioned on sturdy rail sections of the chassis on unibody vehicles and the frame rails on full-frame vehicles. Do not locate the stands on the flat sections of the vehicle floorpan; the weight of the vehicle will likely cause damage to the floor. On vehicles with a solid rear axle, the jack stands can be placed under the axle tubes. Also, avoid placing the stands over brake and fuel lines.

Safety Step

4 Drain Engine Oil

 Remove the drain plug on the oil pain and drain the oil into a drop pan. Some builders do this after the engine is removed, but doing it at this stage prevents the likelihood of leaking when the engine is at an extreme angle during extraction.

5 Drain Coolant and Remove Radiator Hoses

Coolant that drains out of the radiator petcock and hoses is certainly not the last of the liquid in the either the engine or radiator. More will spill from the radiator and engine when they're removed. Coolant draining should begin with the disconnection of the lower radiator hose (seen here), which allows gravity to take care of the bulk of the work. Use a large, wide pan to catch the coolant, as it will spill out quickly and likely splash.

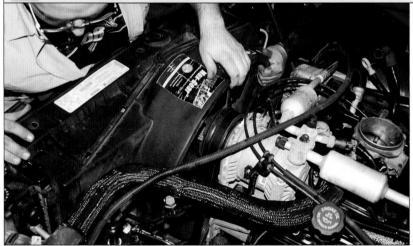

After the radiator has drained, the hoses can be disconnected from the engine and removed. More coolant will drain from the cylinder block, so the drain pain should be positioned below the engine. Again, the coolant will spill out quickly and splash off engine components, so you should be prepared for the ensuing mess.

6 Remove Fan Shroud and/or Cooling Fan

Most late-model vehicles have electric cooling fans, while trucks mostly have engine-driven cooling fans. Regardless of the fan type, it should be removed prior to removing the radiator. Unbolting an engine-driven fan usually requires first the removal of a plastic or sheetmetal fan shroud that is mounted to the radiator. Here, the fan shroud of a vehicle with an engine-driven fan is removed. On some vehicles it is possible to remove the engine with the fan still attached, but the radiator must be moved to prevent the fan from cutting into it during removal. Whenever possible, it is recommended to remove the fan from the engine. Electric fans are typically mounted to the radiator and also require the disconnection of an electrical connector.

This electric cooling fan has a self-contained shroud. It only needs to be unbolted from the radiator and removed. Electric fans also require the disconnection of an electrical connector. As most electric fans use plastic or nylon fan blades, they should be inspected for chips, cracks, or other damage. Typically, the fan blades accumulate a lot of dirt and grime, too, so they should be cleaned prior to re-installation in the vehicle.

7 Remove Radiator

Removal of the radiator frees up "wiggle room" for the engine during the extraction, and it is also protected from damage should the engine inadvertently move forward during the extraction. In addition, it provides an opportunity to inspect the radiator for damage, such as crushed cooling fins, pinhole leaks, etc. The coolant drain pan should be located beneath the radiator during its removal because more coolant will certainly drain from it. Removal of the radiator provides more room for maneuvering the engine during its extraction, and it also prevents damage to the delicate cooling fins. It will likely have more coolant to be drained, too. After removal, the radiator should be inspected for damage from road debris.

Documentation Required

8 Disconnect Heater Hoses

The heater hoses, of course, also carry coolant, and after the radiator has been drained and removed, the coolant drain pan should be positioned under the engine where the heater hoses are located. More working space under there may be freed up by removing the heater hoses completely by also disconnecting them where they meet the firewall.

9 Remove Air Cleaner Assembly and/or Air Intake Tract

The air intake system must be disconnected from the engine because late-model systems typically use a remote-mounted filter box connected to the engine via a flexible intake tube. The air filter box doesn't require removal (unless doing so frees up working space), but the intake tube does. On fuel-injected engines with remote-mounted air cleaner assemblies, the air intake tract must be disconnected from the air cleaner. In most cases, removal of the intake system is as simple as loosening the two ends of the air tract—one at the engine inlet (throttle body) and the other at the air cleaner box—and pulling it off the engine.

Important!

10 Remove Air Cleaner

For engines with carburetors or TBI-type fuel-injection systems that use conventional, engine-mounted air cleaners, removal of the air cleaner assembly frees up the space necessary to disconnect the fuel line and other electrical connections beneath it. The carburetor or throttle body should be covered with a clean rag or similar item to prevent debris from falling into the engine after the air cleaner has been removed.

11 Disconnect Throttle Cable

Generally located on the driver's side of a carburetor or on the outside of a throttle body, the throttle cable should be unhooked and carefully moved aside. Whether on a carburetor, TBI-injection system or port-type-injection system, the throttle cable is typically attached in a similar fashion; the cable mechanism pops off a ball stud-type fastener. A firm tug is all that's required to disconnect it. Some engines may also incorporate a locking ring for the fastener. Nylon ties can be used to secure it out of the way of other components during the extraction procedure. If possible, it should be secured to the inner fender panel or firewall, so that it won't snag on the engine during removal.

Special Tool

12 Disconnect All Fuel Lines

On carbureted and TBI engines, the fuel line attaches to the carburetor or throttle body. The fuel line on a port-fuel-injected engine attaches at the end of a fuel rail that feeds all of the injectors. Fuel-injected engines may also have a fuel-return line that also requires disconnection. Most contemporary fuel systems use fuel lines that incorporate a positive locking ring, which must be pried up and/or off for removal. Some engines require a specialized removal tool. The fuel line connection of this typical port-injected engine (see photo) feeds into a pressure regulator attached to the fuel rail. The fuel line's locking clip on this engine needs only to be pried up for disconnection. Some systems require a special tool to disconnect the fastener.

Documentation Required

13 Disconnect Electrical Connectors

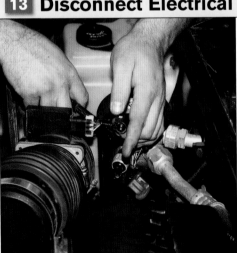

There are too many to list here and they vary from vehicle to vehicle, so it is important to use a service manual as a reference. While most connections may seem self-explanatory during the removal stage, they can prove confusing during re-assembly, so it is a good idea to label many of the connections. In addition, there are numerous single-wire connections for sensors, such as the oil pressure, coolant temperature, etc.

Here is a brief list of major connections to check during the removal stage: Primary ECM wiring harness and supporting harnesses, sensors (oil pressure, coolant temperature, etc.), electric fan switch, ignition system, mass air meter, fuel system harness, idle air control, air conditioning harness.

Important!

14 Secure Wiring Harness

Here's a valuable tip: Use nylon ties to secure wiring looms and harnesses to the chassis and/or firewall after they've been disconnected. This keeps the engine compartment clutter-free and provides unimpeded space for the engine during extraction.

15 Remove Front Accessories

They vary from vehicle to vehicle, but these are the engine-driven components, such as the alternator, mounting brackets, serpentine belt tensioner(s), and the like. First loosen the drive belt(s) to remove the engine's front accessories. On this older, V-belt design, a bolt holding the alternator is loosened on an adjustable bracket in order to provide slack on the belts. Later-type serpentine-belt systems require changing pressure on a tensioner to loosen the belt.

Important!

16 Disconnect Air Conditioning and Power Steering Pumps

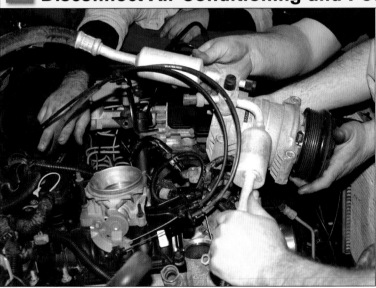

These components are typically mounted to the front engine accessory drive, too, but each features sealed contents that makes outright removal problematic. For the air conditioning system, it is unlawful to discharge the refrigerant, so simply unhooking the hoses and pulling out the pump isn't an option. That leaves two choices: Having the system professionally evacuated prior to removal, or carefully unbolting the compressor from the accessory drive and setting it aside in the engine compartment with all of the hoses connected. Most builders find there is sufficient room in the engine compartment to set aside the air conditioning compressor, but heavy-duty nylon ties will likely be required to support the system and keep it out of the way when the engine is lifted out of the car. The issue with the power steering pump is its fluid lines, which link the pump with the steering rack. Like the air conditioning compressor, it can be unbolted from the accessory drive and set aside in the engine compartment and secured with tie wraps. Care must be taken to avoid excessive play with the pump because the lines typically do not have much "give," which could cause a fluid leak.

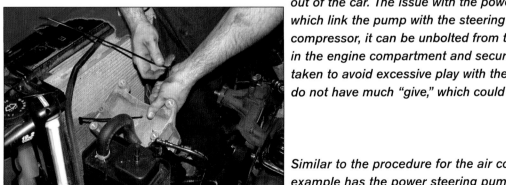

Similar to the procedure for the air conditioning compressor, this example has the power steering pump and its bracket tied to the front chassis of this Chevy Suburban. Caution must be used to prevent the hydraulic fluid hoses from bending far enough to cause a leak.

17 Remove and/or Disassemble Intake Manifold

Opinions vary on whether the intake manifold requires removal prior to the engine's extraction, but many vehicles require disconnection of at least some components of the manifold assembly to provide unimpeded cross-engine clearance for the shop crane's lifting chain. Although some service manuals call for the entire manifold to be removed, others call for the manifold to be used as a lifting point. Generally, it is easier to remove the engine of port-fuel-injected vehicles that feature a tall, multi-piece intake manifold that wraps over the top of the engine, a design usually used with inline-type engines. In this photo, the top section of the engine's intake system is removed to provide better access for the lifting chain, starting with the throttle body. After that, the upper section of the manifold is removed, but it's not necessary to remove the lower section. Holes in the intake system created when the manifold is disassembled should be plugged with, at least, a clean rag.

It shouldn't be necessary to remove a carburetor or TBI-system throttle body on so-equipped vehicles, nor the intake system of V-type engines with a port-style injection system. The manifolds of these engines are typically sufficiently low enough so as not to present an interference problem with the lifting chain.

18 Disconnect Starter and Ignition System

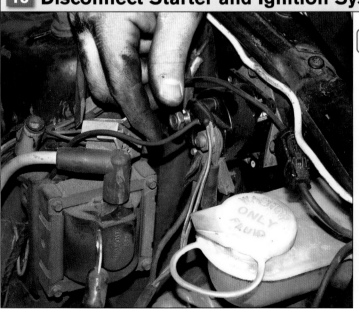

Systems vary among vehicles, but, generally speaking, the starter is disconnected from the vehicle's power source and so is the ignition system. Some vehicles use a remote-mounted ignition coil that is located on the inner fenders or firewall, requiring the coil-to-distributor wire to be removed. Some vehicles—Ford models, in particular—feature a remote-mounted solenoid (seen here). The starter must be disconnected from it. Other vehicles use a starter that incorporates the solenoid. Also noteworthy in this photo is the remote-mounted ignition coil, seen to the left of the solenoid. The coil wire from it must be disconnected from the distributor. For systems that have the coil mounted on the engine, it is only necessary to disconnect the coil from the ignition system; the coil itself does not require removal.

19 Disconnect All Chassis Ground Straps

Almost every vehicle has a wide, flat, braided-steel ground strap that links the engine and the chassis. Typically, the strap is located at the rear of the engine and bolted to the firewall. It is an easy component to overlook during the removal process, so make a concerted effort to disconnect it. The engine of many vehicles also has the negative battery cable grounded directly to the engine, meaning it must be disconnected, too. The engine-to-body ground is not always easy to spot because it can be located very low in the engine compartment. It only needs to be disconnected at the engine; it can remain attached to the body during the engine rebuild process.

20 Disconnect Exhaust System

The extent of the exhaust removal depends on whether the transmission will be removed. If the transmission is removed, you need to determine how much the exhaust system impedes extraction. At the very least, the exhaust pipe(s) must be disconnected at the exhaust manifold(s). For most vehicles, it is not necessary to remove the exhaust manifolds to extract the engine. If it appears the exhaust system impedes the transmission's removal, more of the system requires disconnection and/or removal. Minimally, the exhaust system must be unbolted from the engine's exhaust manifold(s). If the transmission is to be removed, too, the exhaust system should be inspected to gauge whether it will be an impediment toward the transmission's removal. In this photo, the "Y-pipe" that connects both sides of a V-8 engine's exhaust manifolds has been unhooked where it meets the manifolds. And because the transmission is not being removed, the exhaust system can remain in its original position.

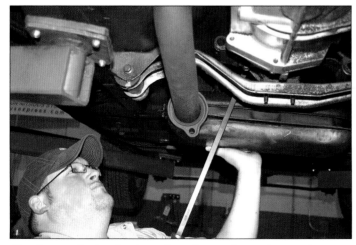

The four-cylinder Ford engine shown throughout this chapter has an exhaust system that crosses under the transmission and transmission crossmember. Because the transmission will be removed with the engine, the exhaust system is disconnected and removed.

Here, the Ford's exhaust system is unhooked after the catalytic converter. The converter is part of a larger assembly that includes the "down pipe" from the exhaust manifold and will also have to be removed.

21 Disconnect Transmission

Perform this procedure only if the transmission is to remain in the vehicle. For vehicles that will not have the transmission removed or, at least, the transmission will not be removed with the engine, the transmission is unhooked where the engine and bellhousing meet. Preparation must be made to support the transmission after the engine is removed, typically with a jack or jack stand positioned at the bottom of the transmission. If the transmission is to remain in the car for the duration of the engine rebuilding process, a sturdy support system for the transmission is needed, such as a piece of wood that straddles the chassis and holds the front of the transmission or the use of several heavy-duty, flexible straps to hold up the transmission. Disconnecting the engine from the transmission can be an awkward procedure because the bellhousing bolts are typically hard to reach. On the Chevy Suburban seen here, professional help was needed to reach all of them. The at-home builder may find it easier, in cases like this, to remove the engine and transmission as an assembly.

22 Disconnect Transmission from Chassis

Perform this procedure only if the transmission is to be removed with the engine. The transmission must be unencumbered from drivetrain and chassis components in preparation for removal. This includes, but is not limited to: speedometer cable, vehicle speed sensor, shifter and/or clutch mechanism, and wiring harness connector(s). Vehicles with floor-mounted shifters (automatic or manual transmission) require the removal of the shifter. This is generally done from the vehicle's interior and may require disassembly of the center console. On manual-transmission vehicles, the clutch pedal cable must be disconnected, while all transmissions must have the speedometer cable, vehicle speed sensor, and other electronic connections unhooked. In this photo, the clutch cable has been disconnected.

23 Disconnect the Shifter

The shifter inside the vehicle must also be removed in order to remove the transmission. This internal-rail-type shifter for a manual transmission simply unbolts and pulls up and out, while other transmissions require considerably more work. Automatic-transmission shifters can be particularly difficult, and the service manual should be consulted.

Important!

24 Remove Driveshaft in Rear Drive Vehicles

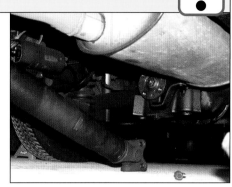

Perform this procedure only if the transmission is to be removed. A simple but somewhat awkward procedure, the driveshaft requires removal before the transmission can be extracted. Generally, this procedure is accomplished by unbolting four fasteners where the shaft meets the rear axle, lowering the rear of the shaft, and sliding the front of the shaft out of the transmission. The shaft can be heavy and awkward to maneuver, so care must be taken to prevent damage. The driveshaft is easily unbolted from the rear axle, but the wheels must be prevented from turning.

After the driveshaft is disconnected from the rear axle, it simply slides out of the transmission tailshaft. Steel driveshafts are heavy and can be awkward to maneuver without assistance. Care must be taken to prevent the shaft from dropping to the floor; this can cause damage.

Professional Mechanic Tip

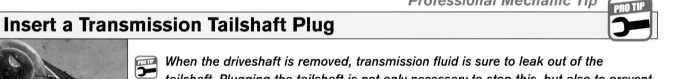

25 Insert a Transmission Tailshaft Plug

When the driveshaft is removed, transmission fluid is sure to leak out of the tailshaft. Plugging the tailshaft is not only necessary to stop this, but also to prevent the fluid from spilling out when the transmission is removed, particularly when the engine/transmission assembly is canted during removal. Although not always easy to find, tailshaft plugs are available and should be used instead of simply stuffing a rag into the shaft—the rag will likely soak through quickly and the spillage will continue. Plastic universal plugs are available, but most auto parts stores do not carry them. They are available from specialty tool retailers and are common finds at automotive swap meets. It may be possible to purchase or borrow a plug from a transmission shop. They may also help locate a shipping plug designed for specific transmissions.

26 Remove Transmission Crossmember

This is a simple procedure that leaves the transmission connected only to the engine, but the transmission likely requires support from a jack stand or block of wood after the crossmember is removed and until the engine/transmission assembly is ready to be pulled.

Once the crossmember is removed, a floor jack supports the rear of the transmission. This enables you to maneuver the transmission more easily during removal.

27 Remove Engine Mount Bolts

Generally, an inline- or V-type engine has two engine mounts that secure it to the chassis or engine cradle. Access to the bolts can be awkward on some vehicles, but removal is as simple as unbolting other fasteners. Likely, the most difficult aspect of unbolting the engine mount bolts is access to the mounts themselves. The mounts on this vehicle, however, were easy to reach without the need for articulating socket attachments or even a deep-well socket, which are required on many vehicles' mounts. Typically, the mount bolts are very long, so the builder should make sure he or she leaves sufficient room to extract them.

Safety Step

28 Locate Factory Lift Brackets and Position Shop Crane Over Engine

 Before attaching the lifting chain, the engine should be checked for factory-installed lift brackets, seen in this photo.

For engines that do not have factory-installed lifting brackets, bolts need to be inserted in the cylinder block, or cylinder head(s), or other components sturdy enough to support the weight of the engine during removal. One of the bolt holes for an exhaust manifold is a common area on an engine to use as a lifting point. The engine in this photo does not have factory lift brackets, so the lift chain is attached in the front on the alternator bracket. At the rear, on the opposite side of the engine, one of the exhaust manifold bolts was removed and reinstalled with the lift chain inserted. Alternate lift points include removing one of the intake manifold bolts or removing the carburetor or TBI throttle body from the manifold and using a special lifting plate that bolts in place of the carburetor or throttle body.

Once these location points are noted, the shop crane and lifting chain are positioned over the engine in preparation for removing the engine. The lift point on the crane should be centered directly over the middle of the engine, and the lifting chain should be attached at diagonal points at the front and rear of the engine, such as the front left corner and the right rear corner. This helps balance the engine's mass as it lifts off the chassis. On front-drive cars in which the transmission is being removed simultaneously with the engine, the lifting chain can be positioned to connect both the engine and transmission for a more balanced removal.

Important!

29 Position Lift Chain

 On this engine, the lift chain has been attached to a factory bracket on the front and via a bolt threaded into the rear of the opposite cylinder head. Note that the lift chain is centered above the middle of the engine, which ensures balance as the engine is lifted off the chassis. When searching for an appropriate lifting point, the builder should use points as close to the top of the engine as possible to keep the engine's weight beneath the lifting chain. This prevents the engine's weight from shifting too much during extraction.

Professional Mechanic Tip

30 Begin Jacking Engine Up and Off Chassis

With the lift chain attached, the engine can be slowly and carefully removed. After the engine is jacked up enough to move it from its chassis mounts, its weight will shift, so care should be taken to prevent it from crashing into chassis components, the power steering pump, etc. It is extremely helpful to have a second person to assist in this part of the project because one person can work the crane and the other can steady the engine as it rises off the chassis. Some builders find it difficult, despite the removal of the engine mount bolts, to pull the engine off the chassis. This can be due to rust, damaged engine mounts, or other reasons. Gentle leverage from a pry bar should be all that's necessary to pop the engine free from the chassis. When the engine has moved a few inches, the clearance of hoses, hard lines, and other engine compartment components should be checked and pulled out of the way, as necessary.

As the engine rises off the chassis, it should be steadied by hand to prevent it from crashing into other components. Slow and steady is the mantra here, with progress checked every few inches to ensure the engine or engine compartment components are not interfering with one another. On vehicles where the transmission remains in the chassis, some gentle prying may be required to separate the engine from the bellhousing.

31 Check Transmission

If the engine and transmission are removed simultaneously in a rear-wheel-drive vehicle, the support at the rear of the transmission should be removed. With the lift chain centered on the engine, the weight of the transmission makes the engine/transmission combination tilt rearward. This is unavoidable and ultimately necessary to pull the assembly out of the engine compartment, but care must be taken to ensure the weight balance isn't too lopsided. Load-leveling tools for shop cranes enable the weight balance of the crane's chain to be shifted. This relatively inexpensive device is very helpful in balancing the engine/transmission assembly during removal.

32 Pull Engine Up and Out of Vehicle

Ultimately, the engine and/or engine/transmission combination moves upward and forward until it clears the front of the vehicle. The safest method is jacking the engine up a few inches and pulling it forward a few inches, repeating this process until it is clear that the engine will pull forward over the front of the car without interference. A tarp or blanket draped over the radiator core support area prevents oil and other fluid from spilling onto the car's painted surfaces, while also serving as a scratch barrier. Here, the engine/ transmission assembly is free and almost out of the vehicle, but the tail-down angle of the transmission means assistance is needed to lift the tailshaft as the engine is pulled forward from the body.

Without the transmission attached, this engine is free and clear of chassis impediments and is ready to be pulled clear of the body. Without the transmission attached to the engine, removing the engine is generally easier, but in some cases, pulling the transmission with the engine is the best course of action.

33 Lower Engine onto Shop Floor or Mount to an Engine Stand

If the transmission is removed with the engine, the assembly needs to be lowered onto the floor so that the transmission can be unhooked. Blocks of wood can be used to steady the engine as it rests on the floor, typically at the high section of the oil pan and on the sides of the engine. If the engine was removed without the transmission, it can be attached directly to an engine stand in preparation for disassembly. In this photo, the engine/transmission assembly was lowered onto garage floor and supported with several pieces of wood. It constituted the final step in the removal process; the next steps involve disconnecting the transmission and preparing the engine for the tear-down process.

ENGINE DISASSEMBLY AND INSPECTION

Tools and Materials Required

- Shop crane
- Engine stand
- Sockets, including deep-wells
- Wrenches
- Screwdrivers / nut drivers
- Timing belt/chain removal tool (overhead-cam engines)
- Breaker bar
- Pulley puller
- Penetrating oil
- Gasket scraper

The teardown procedure involves more than simply disassembling the engine. You must inspect each component as it is removed to determine if the part should be replaced. The part needs to be tagged and bagged according to its condition. The steps are largely the same for inline-type 4-, 5-, and 6-cylinder engines, as well as V-type 6- and 8-cylinder engines. The primary differences when it comes to engine disassembly involve the extra steps necessary to remove parts of the valvetrain and camshaft from a cam-in-block engine, commonly called a pushrod engine.

Regardless of the camshaft configuration, engine disassembly requires patience and attention to detail. Some components, such as the exhaust manifold bolts, crankshaft damper, and even the cylinder head bolts require a great deal of torque to loosen, but care must be taken to prevent damage. In fact, the fasteners of these components should be sprayed with penetrating oil at the very start of the teardown, allowing the oil to soak into the parts, making them easier to remove when the time comes to unbolt them. Some components and fasteners will be replaced during the engine assembly stage of the project, but you should approach the disassembly stage with the attitude that all parts will be re-used. This prevents the unintentional breakage of components that may not be easy or economical to replace.

Removing Stubborn or Broken Fasteners

Some bolts, nuts, and other fasteners may not loosen easily during the disassembly stage, and some may break without relinquishing their hold on the part intended for removal. This problem is more likely to occur with fasteners subjected to extreme heat and little lubrication, such as exhaust manifold bolts and emissions equipment fasteners. These fasteners may also become brittle, making them easier to break. When confronted with a stubborn fastener, you should proceed carefully in order to prevent breaking it.

Spraying the fastener with penetrating oil is the first step. The oil should be left to soak in for a couple of minutes before attempting to remove the fastener. More leverage with a longer-handle tool, such as a breaker bar, can help, but too much torque can easily snap the head off a brittle bolt. Another option is heat applied from a torch. When heated to a glowing-red, a bolt is often easier to remove, but again, care must be take to apply only enough leverage to break loose the fastener; it is still susceptible to breaking.

Sometimes, however, stubborn, brittle fasteners will break. Options are limited if that happens, but dislodging the remnant of the fastener and, ultimately, removing the component can be accomplished with some common methods:

Drill-out the fastener: A bolt with a broken head can be removed by carefully drilling down through the center of bolt with progressively larger drill bit sizes until the bolt essentially disappears or falls apart. Many bolts are made from hardened material, so carbide, cobalt, or similar drill bits should be used with them.

Use an "Easy-Out" tool: This tool, designed for extracting broken fasteners, works much like a drill bit, but has a tapered, conical shape. After a pilot hole is drilled into the fastener, the easy-out-type tool is threaded in slowly (usually with a wrench) until it is firmly wedged in and attached to the fastener. Then, reverse leverage is used to loosen the fastener and remove it. Because the easy-out tool is typically made of harder material than the bolt, care to avoid breaking it must be taken when threading it in. You should proceed very slowly when inserting the easy-out tool.

Clean and tap the bolt hole: After the broken fastener is removed, the bolt hole should be cleaned of all shards, shavings, and debris. Then, the hole should be "chased" with a tap to ensure the threads are clean and undamaged. This is especially important for bolt holes in aluminum parts, because it is easy to gall the bolt-hole threads of the relatively soft material.

Keeping Organized

You should also "tag and bag" as many components as possible, including taking notes on the mounting position or orientation of parts, in order to facilitate a faster, smoother, and error-free assembly later in the project. A part's position may seem obvious during disassembly, but with the literally hundreds of components to deal with during such a project, it is all too easy to forget the original position weeks later, when the engine is assembled. This method complements the act of shooting reference photos to ensure an accurate assembly. As noted in Chapter 1, photos taken at different points during disassembly can serve as references during assembly to confirm mounting position and orientation of components such as wiring looms, hard line fittings, and more.

As the engine comes apart, a few crucial components must be marked and/or noted for their original position, as they must be re-installed exactly. This includes the pistons and rods. Cylinder head bolts and main bearing cap fasteners do not require reinstallation in the original position.

The builder should work smart, too. As seen in the photos of this chapter, it is not necessary to disassemble every component when the removal of larger assemblies accomplishes the job quicker. Examples include removing the intake manifolds with the fuel rails; leaving the injectors intact; and removing the complete cylinder head assembly of an overhead-cam engine, leaving the camshaft and valvetrain intact.

While the outlined procedures of this chapter provide a general guideline for the teardown process, you should supplement this with a shop manual that provides specific information and details regarding the various components unique to your engine.

A Quick Blast

Clean engines are much easier to work on than grimy ones. For this reason, it is worth subjecting the engine and/or transmission to a high-pressure wash prior to the teardown. Additionally, the washed-off engine assembly can provide a more immediate visualization of the source of an oil or coolant leak, or any other malady that contributed to the need for a rebuild.

Spray-on engine degreaser and, usually, a scrub brush are all that's necessary, but a high-pressure wand is a must to blast off the baked-on grime. Yes, it may seem counterintuitive to clean an engine *before* it is rebuilt, but it ultimately makes the processes cleaner, easier, and quicker.

A bad seal on the turbocharger of this engine caused oil to blow over the engine and onto the transmission. The engine was caked in oil, and before the teardown, it was lowered into the back of a pickup for a trip to the local coin-operated do-it-yourself car wash.

A couple of dollars and a few minutes later, the engine and transmission were blasted clean and ready for the teardown process. With the grime blown off the engine, it was much easier to locate all of the fasteners and turned what would have been a filthy teardown process into merely a dirty one.

Of course, the engine block and other parts will receive another, more thorough cleaning at the machine shop.

Check for Damage

If the rebuild project was initiated by an engine failure or a severe, performance-debilitating condition, you should pay particular attention to discovering the cause of the problem through evidence seen during the disassembly. A blown head gasket or spun bearing, for example, is easy enough to confirm once the cylinder head has been removed. Other evidence, such as a burned piston, may be easy to find, but it may only be a *result* of a problem, not the *cause*. Some basic detective work, such as talking with professional engine rebuilders or scanning online forums or blogs, may help you discover a common condition that leads to a specific engine's failure.

Defective cylinder head castings or head gaskets, for example, can be a common occurrence that is shared within an engine line. Knowing this information helps the builder attack the rebuild project with the knowledge to avoid assembling the "new" engine with replacement parts that may cause another failure condition.

If no common problem can be found to explain a failure, additional detective work is required. For example, a lean condition (too much air, not enough fuel) likely caused the burned piston, which could be traced to a defective fuel injector or pressure regulator.

Worn-out engines that did not fail prior to the rebuild should also be inspected for accumulated sludge, wear, or other conditions that could be addressed during the rebuild process. In some cases, simple procedures or replacement parts can be used to avoid a similar condition once the engine is rebuilt. But regardless of the reasons for rebuilding the engine, it should be inspected during the teardown to eliminate a repeated condition once the engine is back in the vehicle.

Transmission Removal

The first steps involve separating the transmission from the engine. The process is largely the same for both manual and automatic transmissions, although there are a few more steps involved with the manual transmission. The transmission and the transmission bellhousing are typically separate components, whereas the automatic transmission is generally attached to the engine as a single component. Also, the clutch must be removed from a manual transmission, and there is no comparable step with an automatic. These steps aren't required if the transmission was not removed as part of the engine assembly. In that case, the engine can be moved, after the flywheel or flexplate is removed, directly to the engine stand.

The steps outlined hereafter describe the teardown process of an engine with a connected transmission. In most cases, the fluid must be drained from a manual transmission. This prevents the fluid from spilling on the floor when the transmission is moved. And while most transmissions can be surely plugged to prevent leakage, draining the fluid encourages you to re-fill the

The need for an engine rebuild was quickly discovered on this supercharged engine when a foreign object was sucked into the engine, destroying the supercharger impeller. The metal shards that were flung off the supercharger were drawn into the engine, damaging the pistons and cylinder walls.

transmission with fresh, new fluid. If an automatic-equipped combination has recorded high mileage, it is also a good idea to drain the old and add fresh fluid.

The following steps provide a general guideline to the procedures involved in the removal of a manual transmission. You should consult a service manual for model-specific variances. Builders whose engine is already separated from the transmission can skip this section and start with the "Engine Disassembly" section.

1 Prepare Engine/ Transmission Assembly

In preparation for the teardown, the engine and transmission are supported on the garage floor. The shop crane is required for a couple more steps, so it is not necessary to disconnect the lift chain at this point.

2 Drain Transmission Fluid

Important!

The teardown begins with the removal of the transmission, starting with draining the transmission fluid (manual transmission). The easiest method involves tilting the front of the engine with the shop crane, so that the fluid runs out of the transmission tailshaft and into a drain pan. If you do not intend to inspect, repair, or replace the fluid in the transmission, it is not necessary to drain the fluid, but care must be taken to ensure it doesn't leak out of the tailshaft.

3 Support Transmission with a Floor Jack

With the transmission fluid drained and support from a floor jack, the transmission is prepared for removal. This allows you to easily pull the transmission away from the engine after it is disconnected. The shop crane is required with this step, as it holds the engine/transmission assembly on a level plane after the floor jack is moved into position.

4 Unbolt Transmission

Unbolt the transmission from the bellhousing (manual transmission); automatic transmissions are typically attached directly to the engine and must be unbolted there. Tight confines may make it difficult to use a standard ratchet on some transmission bolts. A combination of standard sockets, swivel-head attachments, or open-end wrenches may be required.

Important!

5 Disconnect Transmission

⚠ Separate the transmission from the bellhousing (manual transmission) or engine (automatic transmission). The transmission is adequately supported and easily pulled away from the engine and bellhousing with a floor jack. It can be lifted from the jack by hand, but heavier automatic transmissions typically require a shop crane for moving them to a storage area during the engine-rebuild process. Care must be taken to prevent damaging the manual transmission input shaft as the transmission is pulled away from the engine and bellhousing. Automatic transmissions are generally much heavier than manual gearboxes and may require additional support during the separation procedure. The transmission can be set aside for the remainder of the engine teardown process. NOTE: With some automatic transmissions, it may be necessary to remove the engine starter prior to disconnection of the transmission from the engine.

6 Remove Starter

The starter is often bolted to the bellhousing, so its disconnection is required prior to the removal of the bellhousing. The starter is easily removed with the engine out of the vehicle, but is generally a heavy component. Care must be taken to prevent dropping it after it is unbolted from the engine and bellhousing.

7 Unbolt and Remove Bellhousing

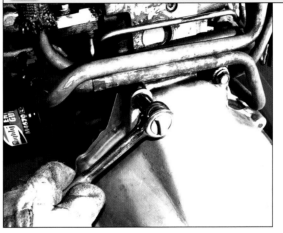

When removing the bellhousing fasteners, you should check both sides of the bellhousing flange because some of the bolts are affixed from the backside, as well as the "front" of the bellhousing (seen here).

After it is unbolted, the bellhousing is carefully removed to ensure it is not caught or snagged on a component underneath it. When it is removed, the clutch pressure plate, clutch disc, and flywheel are exposed.

8 Remove Clutch and Pressure Plate

Unbolt and Remove the Clutch and Pressure Plate. The pressure plate and clutch are held onto the flywheel with bolts located on the perimeter of the pressure plate. The pressure plate is bolted to the flywheel and may require some muscle to loosen, as the bolts were likely installed with thread sealer. Generally, loosening the perimeter bolts is a simple procedure.

9 Remove Pressure Plate and Clutch Disc

The pressure plate and clutch disc are pulled off together. Care must be taken not to drop the clutch disc during removal, if it is to be re-used, but in most cases the clutch disc and pressure plate will be replaced, so the removed items can be discarded.

Engine Disassembly

The following steps cover the basic procedures for disassembling overhead-cam-type or cam-in-block inline and V-type engines. Because components and steps vary among different engines, a shop manual is an essential companion to this list, providing specific component information and/or removal steps. Most of the accompanying photos in this section depict the disassembly of an overhead-cam inline 4-cylinder engine.

Critical Inspection

10 Inspect Clutch Disc for Wear

In most cases, the clutch disc should be replaced during the reassembly stage of the project. It isn't necessary if it had been replaced only shortly before the engine rebuild project commenced. But even with a planned replacement, the old disc should be inspected to ensure its wear was even and consistent. Odd wear patterns or gouges in the friction material could indicate a more serious transmission problem.

11 Remove Flywheel or Flexplate

The flywheel (manual transmission) or flexplate (automatic transmission) is unbolted from the crankshaft flange. It is generally easier to do this before the engine is mounted on an engine stand because the stand can impede clearance or access.

Safety Step

12 Attach Engine Stand Mounting Bracket to Cylinder Block

The engine stand mounting bracket is fastened to the engine block using the automatic-transmission or manual-transmission bellhousing bolt holes. The attaching bolts need to be long enough to pass through the mounting fingers of the bracket and thread into the engine block at least a quarter of an inch.

---

13 Mount Engine on Stand

The shop crane is used to position the engine and attachment bracket in line with the receiver part of the engine stand. Because of its lighter weight, it is typically easier to push the engine stand onto the bracket. The weight of the engine will likely pull down on the stand, which is normal. When the engine and stand are mated, a locking pin holds the engine in the desired position.

Documentation Required

14 Remove External Accessories and Components

On the Ford four-cylinder engine used primarily in this book, engine disassembly started with the removal of the starter cable.

15 Remove Engine Mounting Brackets

Mounting brackets were simply unbolted and placed aside, but as with all of the components to be re-used in the project, they are ultimately stored in a box with other engine parts. Smaller components were placed in plastic bags and tagged with descriptive information.

16 Remove Large Hoses and Hard Lines

The early removal of large hoses (heater hoses) and hard lines makes the disassembly procedure easier. Because they tend to wrap around the engine, removal increases access to the rest of the engine assembly.

Documentation Required

17 Photograph the Position of the Components

The fittings of some hard lines require exact repositioning during the reassembly process. One way to ensure a more accurate assembly is to take reference photos of the fittings prior to removal. The position of many parts may seem obvious during disassembly, but that isn't the case when it is time to reassemble the engine days or weeks later.

The engine primarily photographed in this book was equipped with a turbocharger. It was disconnected from the engine and removed as a single unit with the exhaust manifold. The turbo unit will be separated from the manifold later.

18 Remove Exhaust Manifolds

With the heater hoses and other large hard lines removed, access to the rest of the exhaust side of the engine is greatly enhanced.

The removal of the exhaust manifolds can be one of the most difficult steps of the disassembly process because the manifold bolts are subjected to extreme heat, which can make them very hard to loosen. Spray the bolts with penetrating oil and let the oil soak in for a few moments before attempting to remove them. In fact, you should anticipate the difficulty with the manifolds and spray the bolts with oil as soon as the engine is secure on the stand. This gives the penetrating oil time to soak into the threads while other components are removed ahead of the manifolds. Care must be taken to avoid breaking the bolt heads, which is very easy to do with brittle bolts. Stubborn bolts can be heated up with a torch, which may help break them loose. They should be heated until the heads glow cherry red before attempting to turn them.

19 Remove Intake Manifold/Fuel-Rail Assembly

On most late-model vehicles with port-style fuel injection, the intake manifold—whether on an inline engine or V-type engine—can be removed with the fuel injectors and fuel rail intact. This reduces the steps in the disassembly proce-dure. Unless there is a reason to suspect fault in the injectors or fuel system, there is no need to remove the components from the manifold.

Here's the intake removal of a typical V-type engine, with the upper section of the manifold and throttle body still intact. On this engine, it was easier to remove the mani-fold after the valve covers were removed. That isn't the case on all V-type engines; in fact, most intakes can be removed with the valve covers in place.

Professional Mechanic Tip

20 Remove Distributor

The distributor comes out next, but not before its position is noted. Often, a marker is used to scribe a line from the distributor to the engine block, but because the rebuilt engine will be painted, the mark will disappear. So the end of a flat-blade screwdriver is used to scribe the mark and slightly scratch into the metal of both the distributor and engine block. This provides a reference mark when it's time to re-install the distributor.

NOTE: On some engines—the Chevy small-block V-8 (and GM 4.3L V-6) being the biggest example—the distributor must be removed prior to removing the intake manifold, as the distributor passes through a hole in the manifold. Also, many late-model engines are equipped with distributorless ignition systems, meaning there is no conventional distributor to remove.

21 Remove Front Drive Accessories

These items include the pulleys and brackets for the alternator, water pump, and various tensioners. These can be generally unbolted and removed without the need of a pulling tool.

After the alignment mark is etched into the engine block and distributor housing, the distributor can be pulled up and out of the engine. Care should be taken to avoid turning the distributor shaft or rotor after it is removed. If the shaft or rotor is moved, the engine may run rough on start-up because timing will be off.

22 Tag and Bag

As the bolts, fasteners, and other small parts start to come off the engine, it is a very wise idea to tag and bag them. This eliminates confusion during the assembly process and ensures the correct bolts are used with each component.

23 Remove Water Neck and/or Water Pump

Water pump design and placement varies greatly among engines. On this Ford engine, the water inlet neck is located in front of the cylinder head (shown being removed here), and the water pump is accessible only after removing the timing cover.

Here, the timing cover is removed, revealing the water pump on the left-hand side of the engine.

With the timing cover removed, the water pump is easily unbolted and removed. Again, all engines are configured differently, so the procedures noted here and in the previous photos and captions may not correspond with other engines, but the general steps are similar.

24 Remove Balancer/Crankshaft Pulley Bolt

The removal of the balancer is necessary on many engines to allow removal of the timing cover, and, consequently, access to the timing gear. This was not the case on the 2.3-liter Ford engine noted in the previous photos. Removing the crankshaft pulley/balancer often requires a pulling tool that can be rented or purchased at almost any auto parts store, but the tools and removal methods vary among engines. Consult the shop manual for specific removal instructions and follow them exactly. Do not use heat to loosen a stubborn balancer because heat can damage the balancer and crankshaft. On this late-model GM V-8 engine, a tool is threaded onto the end of the crankshaft hub in order to pull off the balancer.

Special Tool

25 Remove Balancer/Pulley

26 Remove Timing Cover

Using the crankshaft for leverage, the balancer/pulley is pulled off the crankshaft hub as the tool is turned. Another common removal tool is a three-jaw puller that grasps the pulley from behind, again using the crankshaft for leverage. Auto parts stores and other outlets that rent pullers should have a reference guide to ensure the puller is suitable for a specific engine.

The timing cover on most engines is easily removed after the crankshaft pulley and/or balancer has been removed. It may be more complicated on V-type overhead-cam and dual overhead-cam engines, but the general procedure is similar.

27 Remove Timing Belt or Chain

On cam-in-block engines (also known as overhead-valve engines), the timing belt/chain is removed by simply unbolting the timing gear on the camshaft, after which the gear and chain will slip off. The crankshaft gear can be pulled off after the crankshaft has been removed from the engine. On overhead-cam engines, the timing gear generally uses a tensioner that must be loosened or removed so the timing belt has enough slack to slip off the gears. Multiple-cam engines and overhead-cam V-type engines typically have a regimented removal process that should be followed to the letter, as proscribed by the shop manual. This can involve a special cam removal/ installation tool, too. After releasing the tensioner on this single overhead-cam engine, the timing belt was loosened enough for it to be easily slipped off the camshaft and crankshaft gears.

28 Remove Auxiliary Shaft and/or Balance Shaft (If Equipped)

Some engines, such as the Ford 4-cylinder seen throughout this chapter, also incorporate an auxiliary shaft or engine-driven balance shafts. It should be removed along with the timing gear. In the case of the Ford engine, the auxiliary shaft drives the distributor. Its removal starts with the unbolting of the shaft's drive gear.

The camshaft-like auxiliary shaft is housed behind a cover. After the cover is removed, the auxiliary shaft is easily pulled out of the engine. The procedure is similar for balance shafts.

29 Remove all Valve Covers

Removing the valve covers (also known as rocker covers) is a simple procedure, involving only the removal of the cover bolts and the lifting off of the covers. Gentle prying with a flat-blade screwdriver is often needed to break the seal formed between the cover and gasket. Care should be taken to pry gently and avoid bending the sealing rail of the valve cover. NOTE: Builders of overhead-cam engines can skip from here to step 33.

30 Loosen Rocker Arms and Remove Pushrods

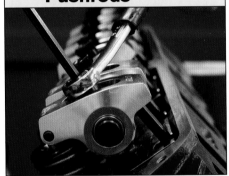

On cam-in-block engines, the rocker arms must be loosened enough to move them to one side in order to allow the pushrods beneath to be pulled out of the engine. If undamaged, the pushrods are reusable.

31 Remove Valve Lifters

After the pushrods on a cam-in-block engine are removed, the valve lifters can be extracted from the cylinder block. On some engines, this is as easy as grasping the lifters by hand, but using hooked-nose pliers or needle-nose pliers will also help pull them free of the cylinder block. Solid lifters that do not have an inner edge to grasp can be removed gently with adjustable pliers.

Professional Mechanic Tip

32 Remove Camshaft

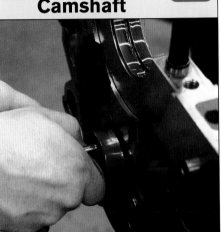

With the lifters removed on a cam-in-block engine, the camshaft can be pulled out of the block. Because the lifters are out of the way, there should not be impediments to damage the lobes as the camshaft is pulled out of the cylinder block. There are camshaft removal/installation tools, but often camshafts that cannot be simply pulled out by hand can be extracted by simply threading a bolt into the end of the cam where the timing chain sprocket attaches. Then, the bolt can be used as leverage to pull out the camshaft.

Using a Valvetrain Organizer

As progress on engine disassembly reaches the valvetrain, many builders find it more convenient to keep track of the components with an organizer tray. This tray has a dedicated space for all of the components, including the rocker arms, valvesprings, pushrods, retainers, etc. Components for each cylinder are stored together, too. These valvetrain organizer trays are available from many engine supply retailers, such as Summit Racing (summitracing.com) and Speedway Motors (speedway motors.com), and typically cost between $20 and $30.

Important!

33 Loosen and Remove Cylinder Head Bolts

Loosening the cylinder head bolts typically requires the leverage of a breaker bar or similar tool. Care should be taken to avoid damaging valvetrain components when turning the breaker bar or wrench. The builder should break loose all of the bolts before going back to remove them.

34 Lift Off Both Cylinder Heads

Like the valve covers, the cylinder heads may require some prying to break the seal between them and the cylinder head gasket. If necessary, pry between the edge of the block or an exhaust port and the head. The prying procedure should be slow and smooth in order to not damage the head; you should use only a little muscle at first, applying more pressure as needed. Once freed, however, the heads should pull straight off the block without interference. Cylinder heads, even aluminum heads, are heavy, so you should have a clear path to the bench or wherever the head is to be placed after it is removed.

35 Scrape Off All Cylinder Heads Gaskets

The head gasket can generally be scraped off easily, although an amount of residue of the gasket material is bound to stick to the cylinder deck surface. It is not imperative to scrape off every remnant of material if the block will be cleaned in a hot-tank. If, however, the builder does not plan to have the deck professionally cleaned, it is very important to remove every bit of gasket material. Lacquer thinner or similar fluid can be used to loosen stubborn pieces.

Documentation Required

36 Remove Sensors from Block and/or Heads

Remove sensors and other components from the cylinder block and/or cylinder heads, including oil pressure sending unit, coolant temperature sensor, oil temperature sensor, etc. There is generally not a rule about when to remove sensors, switches, and sending units located on the engine, but each should be removed and stored for re-use. You should consult the shop manual to check whether any of the sensors require replacement with a new unit after removal. Every sensor that is to be re-used (some may be replaced) should be bagged and tagged. Taking reference photos of the correct locations in the block is smart, too.

37 Remove Oil Pan

Similar to the valve covers and cylinder heads, gently pry the oil to break the seal of the gasket. Use a gasket scraper or similar tool for this procedure. The somewhat-thin construction of the stamped steel material of many pans means care must be taken to avoid bending the perimeter flange. Some oil pans are made of cast aluminum, which won't bend like stamped steel, but the material is easily gouged. This could create a leak path, so care must be taken to prevent damage to these pans, as well.

38 Remove Oil Pump Pick-Up Tube and/or Oil Pump

The oil-pump pick-up tube is generally fastened to one of the main bearing caps. You need to note the specific location to ensure the proper main-cap torque procedure during the assembly phase of the project. A photo of the pump prior to removal is the way to go.

39 Remove Crankshaft Timing Gear

If it hasn't already been removed, the crank's timing gear should be pulled off the hub. This is relatively easy and requires no pullers or other tools. If it is stuck, a light tap on the back of it with a mallet should be all that's required to break it loose.

Documentation Required

40 Loosen and Remove Main Bearing Cap Bolts

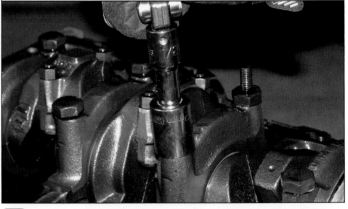

A breaker bar may be required to loosen the main bearing cap bolts or nuts. They can be removed without worry about being matched with the cap because main cap bolts don't have to be returned to the original cap during re-assembly. However, notes must be taken to ensure the builder knows the proper location of any varied fasteners, such as the oil pump pick-up tube fastener.

41 Remove Main Bearing Caps

To remove the main caps on most engines, a gentle tap with a rubber mallet or dead-blow mallet is usually required. The builder should tap only hard enough to "pop" the cap free from its seat. Then, the cap is pulled off and its bearing is removed from it.

42 Mark Main Caps

Important!

Most engines' main caps are marked or cast with indicators that identify their position on the engine, such as those seen here from the Ford 2.3-liter engine (the indicators are numbered "arrow heads," with the points indicating the direction of the front of the engine). Mark the caps if they do not have factory indicators—it is extremely *important* to match the caps with their original bearing position.

43 Remove Rear Seal (If Necessary)

This task may not be required on all engines because some seals are affixed differently. But for those with a seal such as the one shown here, it is easily pulled off the rear of the crankshaft.

44 Loosen Connecting Rod Bolts and Remove Rod Caps

With the main caps removed, work turns to loosening the connecting rod caps. The crankshaft is easily turned to position the rod caps in the best position for removal. A standard ratchet/socket combination should be all that's required to loosen the bolts, although some bolts may have 12-point heads and require a matched socket.

Similar to the main bearing caps, gentle tapping with a rubber mallet or dead-blow mallet may be required to break the rod caps off their seat on the rods.

Once off their seats, the rod caps pull easily off the studs. The bearing can be removed from the cap after it is removed. The bearing should be inspected for unusual wear that could indicate a problem to be addressed during the rebuilding process.

Important!

45 Remove Piston/Rod Assemblies From Cylinders

With the rod caps removed, you can push the rods off the crankshaft, pushing the piston-and-rod assembly up through the cylinder bore and out of the engine. Care must be taken to avoid dinging or damaging the crankshaft and cylinder walls during this procedure. Some builders use pieces of rubber hose on the rod studs to prevent the studs from scratching the crankshaft or cylinder walls. Regardless, the rod should be kept at the center of the cylinder during removal because, even with the studs covered, the rod could still damage or crack the bottom of the cylinder bore.

Safety Step

46 Remove Crankshaft and Main Bearings

With the piston/rod assemblies removed, the crankshaft can be lifted out of the cylinder block. After that, the main bearings are removed, completing the disassembly portion of the project. The bearings should pop out of the main bores by hand and without the assistance of a tool. Do not attempt to rotate the cylinder block after the rod/piston assemblies have been removed and prior to the crankshaft's removal. This may seem like an obvious point, but many absent-minded engine builders have rotated the engine after the main bearing caps have been removed and the crank sits unsecured in the block. As a result, many crankshafts have been ruined (and many toes crushed). Do not make this simple mistake.

With the engine disassembled, the block can be visually inspected for remaining hardware, such as sensors and other components. On this block, the head gasket and an oil cooler housing still require removal. After that, the block is ready for the machine shop.

MACHINE WORK AND CLEAN UP

Unless your home garage is equipped with a milling machine, crankshaft balancer, and other professional machining equipment, you, the do-it-yourself/home-based engine re-builder, will require the services of a machine shop. These professionals will inspect and/or repair engine components to ensure they comply with factory service specifications. This is true even if a budget rebuild is planned with only new piston rings and bearings. A professional inspection is critically important

because most worn items or out-of-spec components aren't discernable to the eye. Also, the engine components must be inspected for damage if the rebuild project was driven by a debilitating condition, such as chronic overheating. This means the cylinder head deck(s) must be examined, as well as the deck-mating surfaces of the cylinder head(s).

In other words, simply installing new main bearings in a cylinder block with a crankshaft that looks fine but needs machine work will

likely cause premature engine wear, or the engine may fail altogether. Most engines with higher mileage or a severe-duty cycle rarely need only new rings and bearings, which is generally a quick fix to coax a couple more years out of the engine. A quality rebuild that will deliver years of service requires a thorough inspection, and likely, more than a little machine work. This is particularly important if the engine has a history of overheating because a severe thermal cycle is the primary cause of

With the engine disassembled, the builder drops off the cylinder block, heads, crankshaft rods, and pistons at his local machine shop.

The builder thoroughly discusses his needs with the machine shop operator. Novice builders can often get good advice from the machine shop for necessary inspections, cleaning, and other operations needed to refurbish the engine parts.

cylinder-block misalignment and distortion.

Many builders, citing time and/or budgetary reasons, enter the rebuild process convinced their engine requires only a fresh set of piston rings and surfaced cylinder heads. As mentioned above, this process will likely provide another few thousand miles of service, but it will not ultimately restore power or longevity. This is even true for engines with a visible crosshatch pattern on the cylinders. According to conventional wisdom, a visible hatch pattern means the cylinder bores are not excessively worn. And while that may be true, the bores should still be inspected for roundness specifications. In addition, cylinder bores are not absolutely round, and this is not visible to the eye. Piston rings and cylinder bores conform to a slightly oblong or oval shape and new rings installed in an un-machined block may cause cylinder sealing problems, leading to oil consumption, lowered compression, and more. Bottom line: If you are seeking long-term performance from the rebuilt engine, you should plan to have the block machined and the cylinder heads surfaced.

At the Machine Shop

Selecting a machine shop can be challenging for the inexperienced re-builder, but ask friends and those at repair facilities for a reputable local establishment. Sometimes it may be the grimiest-looking building in town, but a machine shop that's been in business for a number of years likely has an established and respected reputation. Frankly, bad auto shops don't last very long. A local machine shop is preferred because it affords you the opportu-nity to deliver the components in person and discuss needs and expectations with those who will be doing the work. Sending out the engine parts to a distant facility may be the only option for some re-builders. If that is the only viable option, you should be sure to include detailed written descriptions of the engine and its components, as well as clear instructions on the machine work you want performed. Don't assume the person taking the order over the phone will translate it properly to the technician performing the work.

It's helpful to contact the machine shop prior to dropping off the engine components. This allows you to discuss the project with a representative from the shop and ensure the work will be done in a timely manner. If, for example, the shop is backlogged with work they may not accept your parts immediately, so there's no reason to load up the cylinder block, heads, etc., only to return home and repeat the process when the machine shop is ready for them.

Cylinder Block and Reciprocating Component Inspection and Machine Work

For the best-quality engine rebuild, the work to be done at a machine shop should include:

- Clean the cylinder block and check it for cracks, also known as *Magnafluxing*
- Install camshaft bearings (cam-in-block engines) and freeze plugs
- Inspect the main bearing bores and machine as needed, also known *align-honing*
- Inspect the cylinder block deck(s) and machine as needed, also known as *decking*
- Inspect the cylinder bores and machine as needed, also known as *boring* or *over-boring*
- Inspect the cylinder head deck surface and machine as needed, as known as *milling* or *surfacing*
- Inspect the crankshaft and machine as needed, also known as *turning* and *polishing*
- Inspect the connecting rod bores and machine as needed
- Machine the surface of the flywheel (manual-transmission vehicles)

Machine shops work to order, but after the cylinder block work is completed, most will install freeze plugs (also called core plugs) and spray a coat of paint on the cleaned and machined cylinder block, in order to prevent corrosion.

Do not order an engine rebuild kit until the machine shop has completed its work on the cylinder block and cylinder head(s). This is because the rebuild kit will come with specifically sized pistons, bearings, and other components, and without the machine shop's recommendations, it is impossible to determine whether oversized pistons or crankshaft bearings are needed. The following subsections provide a closer look at the work performed by the machine shop and what you need to know about the procedures.

Cleaning the Cylinder Block
To prepare the cylinder block for inspection and machine work, it must be cleaned to remove years of rust, scale, and grime. Cleaning is generally performed in a hot tank or with a jet-clean process. With the hot tank, the block is immersed in a caustic bath that's heated to approximately 200 degrees F (93 degrees C), which causes the grime

and rust to fall away. After it is removed from the caustic bath, the block is washed. The hot tank is for iron and steel only; aluminum blocks should not be cleaned with this method.

With the jet-clean process, the block is blasted under high pressure with heated water and a cleaning solution, and it is safe for iron, steel, and aluminum. The block is blasted while it spins on a turntable, ensuring all corners are equally blasted. More and more machine shops are using the jet-clean processes because it is a more environmentally friendly alternative to the hot tank.

Like the hot tank method, however, the block is rinsed after the jet-clean process. With all cleaning options, the bolt holes, water passages, and oil passages should be cleaned out with stiff brushes. This prevents grime from collecting in the holes that would otherwise block coolant and/or oil flow. Ask the machine shop if cleaning the block with brushes is part of the basic cleaning procedure. If it isn't, insist the procedure is performed.

Checking for Cracks in the Cylinder Block

Cracks can be formed for a variety of reasons, such as a history of overheating, stress on a high-mileage engine, extreme freezing, and common casting problems within an engine family. Often, cracks will appear in the same area on a family of engines and knowledgeable technicians will know to check the crack-prone areas.

The most common method of checking for cracks involves the use of a tool from Magnaflux; in fact, it is so common that most shops generically refer to block inspections as "Magnafluxing." The Magnaflux tool uses a high-power electromagnet. When the magnetic field is induced (turned on), the technician sprinkles iron powder onto the block. If a crack exists, the powder will immediately collect along the fissure, showing its shape and length.

Other methods of checking for cracks use dyes sprayed on the cylinder block or liquid material that identifies cracks under a black light. A cracked block typically means it must be discarded. Some cracks can

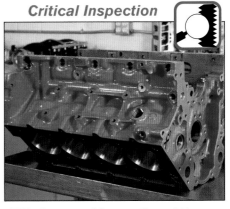

Critical Inspection

A general inspection of the cylinder block should be performed after it has been thoroughly cleaned. The machine shop should also check crack-prone areas on engines whose "family" has a history of cracking or other common defects. The machine shop often finds cracks the builder didn't notice and didn't have the knowledge to search for. Common cracking areas on cylinder blocks include the bottom of the cylinders, the deck surfaces (near the cylinder openings), the front and rear bulkheads, and the valley area between the cylinder banks (V-type engines). The machine shop should also inspect for cracks in or around the water jackets.

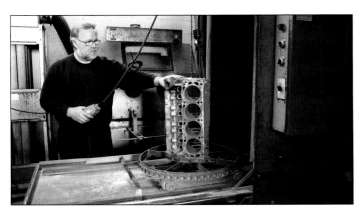

In this photo, a bare cylinder block is loaded into a jet cleaner to remove the grease, scale, and grime. After its time in the cleaner, the block is removed and thoroughly rinsed. Prices vary for this procedure, depending on the method of cleaning, but $100 is a good estimate.

Because the jet cleaner uses less caustic material, machine shops and engine shops are using it more and more. It is also cheaper to operate and requires less cleaning time per block. Also, the jet cleaner is safe for iron, steel, aluminum, and plastic components; the hot tank is used only with iron and steel parts.

be repaired, but generally, if the machine shop finds a significant crack, it's time to find a replacement cylinder block.

Inspecting and Machining the Crankshaft and Camshaft Bores

The crankshaft (main bearing) and camshaft bores must be aligned within, generally, 0.002 to 0.001 inch of the factory specifications. The machine shop measures the size and roundness of the bores, checking for distortion and whether they remain within the acceptable range of the manufacturer's specification range. This is essential to ensuring the crankshaft and camshaft(s) spin true within the bores. While some engines won't require machine work, most minimally worn engines will likely require an "align-hone" procedure.

Align honing lightly machines the main bores, truing them up to ensure they're round. This may require plus-sized main bearings, the size of which won't be known until

the machine shop completes the procedure. This is one of the reasons the re-builder shouldn't order an engine rebuild kit until the machine shop completes its work.

More seriously out-of-spec main bores may require an "align-bore" procedure. This machining process cuts more material out of the block and caps in order to "true" the bores. This procedure requires the use of plus-sized main bearings. Often, the main caps can distort because of stress and/or extreme temperature, such as during overheating. A spun bearing can also require an align-bore job.

During the inspection, the machine shop should also check for wear on the thrust bearing of the main cap, as well as wear on the camshaft bores on overhead-cam engines. Because the camshafts are so far away from the oil pump on an overhead-cam engine, oil can take longer to reach the cam bore during cold starts. Over time, this can damage the journals or bearings.

Inspecting and Machining the Cylinder Block Deck(s)

The cylinder block deck is the top surface along the cylinder bank, where the cylinder head is attached. It must be as flat as possible to ensure a tight, leak-free seal for the head. The deck is subject to warping under

The decking procedure involves locking the block on a fixture below a spinning cutting tool that removes a minute layer of material to leave a flat mating surface for the cylinder head. Only a minimal amount of material should be removed in order to preserve accurate cylinder head fastener alignment and prevent piston-to-valve interference.

Align honing is performed on a rigid fixture with a long honing tool that enables all of the crankshaft bores to be machined simultaneously. The main bearing caps are bolted snugly in place for this procedure, ensuring perfectly round bores.

A look at post-honed crankshaft bores shows a fresh crosshatch pattern. Align honing or align boring may require the use of oversized bearings. The rebuilt engine's bearing size isn't determined until the crankshaft is inspected and/or machined, so the builder should hold off on ordering a rebuild kit until the block's machine work has been finished.

high heat, and its flatness should be checked by the machine shop. Often, the decks of rebuildable cylinder blocks—even if there isn't a history of overheating or other problems—are lightly machined to provide a clean, optimally flat surface. This process, which cuts into the deck surface to level it, is called "decking."

Because decking removes material from the deck surface, it slightly lowers the mounting position of the cylinder head. While it's not a problem for most rebuildable engines, a decking procedure that cuts too much of the surface can alter the mounting geometry of intake manifolds on V-configuration engines. This condition is exacerbated if the deck surface of the cylinder head also is machined.

Additionally, a decked block and/or a machined cylinder head surface can affect the compression ratio of the engine because the removed material effectively shrinks the combustion chamber. It can also

lead to piston-to-valve clearance problems. The vehicle manufacturer has guidelines for machining within interference-free boundaries, and the machine shop should take care to check that its machine work does not exceed those specifications. If the cylinder block (or head) requires cutting behind the manufacturer's specs, the block may not be a good candidate for the rebuild.

Inspecting and Machining the Cylinder Bores

Optimal engine performance requires sealed, leak-free cylinders. Engines that burned oil prior to rebuild or had lowered compression generally had at least one "bad" cylinder, but even seemingly "healthy" engines suffer from cylinder wear over thousands of miles. The conventional wisdom of most backyard mechanics says that if you can still see the crosshatch pattern inside the cylinder bores, you can simply re-ring the pistons and be on your way. Often, that is not the case.

An engine's heat cycles generally affect the roundness of the cylinders and the piston rings. Even the pistons can be affected. New piston rings in a worn, slightly out-of-round cylinder—even one in which the crosshatch pattern is clearly visible—will likely cause oil blow-by, oil burning, and lowered compression. So, it is important to let the machine shop inspect and measure the bores against the manufacturer's specifications.

Some cylinder blocks may only require honing to true up the bores. If this is the case, the original pistons can probably be re-used (after they're cleaned and inspected for cracks) along with new piston rings. More often, the re-builder should plan on having the block slightly over-bored in order to deliver compliant specs. Like decking, over-boring (also called, simply, "boring") involves removing material in order to make the surfaces come into the manufacturer's specifications.

To bore and/or hone an iron block, the machine shop places the

Professional Mechanic Tip

In this photo, a cylinder block is undergoing honing, after having been over-bored. In some cases, a cylinder block may only require a hone procedure to make it suitable for rebuilding. Note the torque plates attached to the block in the photo, which simulate the pressure on the block caused by installed cylinder heads. Boring and honing with torque plates delivers a more accurate cylinder shape and promotes better piston ring fitment and cylinder sealing. Torque-plate honing is not required for most stock-type engine rebuilds, but is a good way of ensuring a tight piston-ring-to-wall relationship.

The shiny reconditioned cylinder bores are visible in this photo. The honing process produces a necessary crosshatch pattern on the cylinders that is essential for achieving a tight seal, retaining oil, and ensuring against oil consumption. Consequently, the bores will have a slightly rough feel to them after this step is completed.

block on a boring machine that will cut the cylinder to the desired size. The honing process uses an abrasive tool to smooth the cylinders, producing the characteristic cross hatch pattern on the cylinder walls. The cross-hatched finish is important because it holds oil on the cylinder

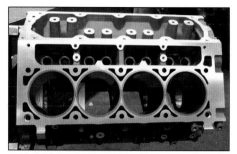

Aluminum cylinder blocks use iron cylinder liners that, on most engines, cannot be over-bored. If honing won't bring the cylinders into spec, they may require replacement. The tight fit required to keep the liners in place means replacing them is time-consuming and expensive. In some cases, it may be less expensive to source a replacement block.

walls. A torque plate may be used during the boring and honing process, as it simulates the distortion of the block when the cylinder heads are installed, promoting a more accurate and tighter cylinder seal when the engine is assembled.

Aluminum cylinder blocks typically have cast iron cylinder liners that can generally be honed but not bored. With luck, an aluminum engine block can get away with a simple honing, but if the machine shop determines more than a hone is required, the alternatives are few and, typically, very expensive—usually involving the removal and replacement of the cylinder liners. If this is required, you may want to consider locating a used replacement block or engine.

Camshaft Bearings and Freeze Plugs

Other tasks that can be accomplished by the machine shop include the installation of camshaft bearings and freeze plugs. The installation of cam bearings in the cylinder block

applies only to cam-in-block (pushrod) engines, while all engine types use freeze plugs, also called freeze-out plugs or core plugs. You can install the freeze plugs at home, but if the machine shop is willing to perform the task inexpensively or as part of their "check and prep" package, you should have it done.

Crankshaft Inspection and Machining

The crankshaft must be inspected for overall straightness, balance, and excessive wear or grooves that may have developed on the main-bearing and rod journals. Extreme thermal cycling, sustained heating, or prolonged high-load conditions can cause the crankshaft to bend, while spun bearings and other issues can create wear on the journals. Typically, a straight, reusable crankshaft with little or no wear on the journals should at least have the journals polished. Minor machine work can bring more severely worn journals into specification but this requires

Camshaft bearings for a cam-in-block are installed with a long tool and a plastic wedge that seats the bearings in the bores. This is not a tool most builders have at home, which is the reason the task is almost always performed at the machine shop. The procedure depicted here is not required for overhead-cam engines with bearing caps similar to main caps. However, some overhead-cam engine cylinder heads have single-piece camshaft "towers" and not removable caps. For those engines, the cam bearings must be installed similarly to the cam-in-block method.

Installing freeze plugs requires little more than a mallet and a reciprocating tool that has the same diameter as the inner diameter of the plug. This ensures the plug is driven straight and square into the block. This procedure can be accomplished at home or at the machine shop.

Critical Inspection

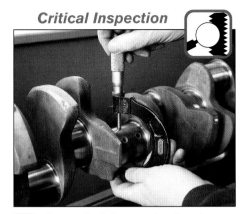

  Crankshaft inspection involves measuring across the journals at the ends and center to check for any variance in diameter. The rods or crankshaft can cause the wear and if the journal isn't within specs all the way across, it will likely require machining (cutting) to bring it into compliance. Also have the thrust flange, keyways, and rear seal surface inspected, as well as the threads on the flywheel flange and nose. With the right tools, these inspections can be accomplished at home; or, the builder can have the machine shop perform them along with their other inspections.

oversized bearings (see "What is a '10/10' Crankshaft?" on page 59).

Crankshafts that are slightly bent can often be straightened and reused, but crankshafts for most engines are relatively inexpensive. If the original crankshaft's straightness is on the borderline of the manufacturer's specifications range, the re-builder should consider replacing it. The machine shop should provide guidance on whether the crankshaft is salvageable.

What is a "10/10" Crankshaft?

There are two types of journals on a crankshaft: the main journals, which turn inside the main bearings of the cylinder block; and the rod journals, which are the areas onto which the connecting rods are mounted. During the inspection and machining process, material may be removed from both types of journals. The machine shop will specify the amount of material removed from each type of journal, typically measuring in thousandths of an inch. This is important because it determines the correct size of the replacement bearings.

So, the common "10/10"-turned crankshaft refers to a crank that has had 0.010 inch removed from the main journals and 0.010 inch removed from the rod journals. Consequently, bearings that are 0.010 inch larger (thicker) are required to maintain the manufacturer's specifications. It is not uncommon, however, to have 0.020 inch removed from the main journals and only 0.010 inch removed from the rod journals—delivering a "20/10"-turned crankshaft.

The crankshaft in the photo didn't require machining, so the machine shop proceeded with polishing the journals. It involves placing the crankshaft on a lathe and lowering a polishing belt onto the journals.

As the crankshaft spins on the lathe, the hand-held polishing tool's belt spins, too, quickly polishing the journals to a mirror finish. The operator simply moves the polishing tool to the next journal to continue the procedure.

Inspecting the Connecting Rod Bores

Similar to the crankshaft and camshaft bore inspections, the big-end (crankshaft) connecting rod bores should be inspected for roundness and wear. Machine work can bring slightly out-of-spec bores into shape, but some bores may also require machining if different-size bearings are to be used with a machined crankshaft.

Machining the Flywheel for Manual-Transmission Vehicles

This is a quick, simple procedure that re-surfaces the flywheel, straightening it and giving the surface more "bite" for the clutch. This isn't necessary for automatic-transmission combinations. The process is similar to the decking procedure for the cylinder block.

"Hanging the Rods": Assembling the Rods and Pistons

With most automotive engines, the pistons and rods are joined with wrist pins that must be pressed into place. In fact, they will likely require a press to be separated, too. Generally, most home garages won't have a press suitable to perform this task, so the machine shop should perform this for you. The exception to this is floating pins that are slipped in place and held on with circular clips; no press is required to fit the pins.

Most machine and engine shops these days use a unique heater device to install press-fit wrist pins. With it, the ends of the rods are heated enough to make them expand slightly. They are then quickly removed from the heater and placed in a fixture, where the pin is then simply pushed into place. As the rod end cools, the pin is locked in place.

At most machine shops, the rods and pistons are joined via the wristpin using a special heater. The heater allows the connecting rod end to expand enough to slip in the pin without a press. The operator must move quickly; if the rod cools too much before the pin is inserted, the pin could get stuck halfway in, causing a big headache for the operator.

Critical Inspection

Like the crankshaft bores, the ends of the connecting rods should be inspected for in-specification roundness and overall wear. Most rods can be machined to bring them into spec. If the engine suffered a catastrophic failure that inducing the rebuild project, the rods should also be inspected for damage, such as cracking or bending.

Critical Inspection

Rod-and-piston assemblies that use floating wrist pins can be easily assembled by hand at the machine shop or in your home shop. The process starts by slipping the pin partially into the piston. If the original pistons are reused, they must be inspected for cracks and other damage that generally occurs at the bottom of the skirts (the broad sides of the piston) or the ring lands (the grooved sections where the rings are located). Even brand-new pistons should be inspected to ensure they weren't damaged during shipping.

Next, the rod is inserted into the piston and the pin is pushed all the way through it and into the opposite side of the piston.

Critical Inspection

Cylinder head surfacing is performed with a cutting tool that operates similarly to the tool used to deck the cylinder block. Only a small amount of material should be removed in order to "true up" the surface and straighten it. Aluminum heads are notorious for warping, particularly when used with a cast iron cylinder block. An overheated condition can easily warp iron heads, too.

Finally, the wrist pin is held in place by circular clips that are installed with the assistance of a flat-blade screwdriver or needle-nose pliers. When using full floating pins, this is all that's required to attach the rods to the pistons.

Cylinder Head Inspection and Machining

The builder has several choices when it comes to the cylinder heads. Among the most basic and lowest-cost options is a simple inspection and light machining of the deck surface. This can be accomplished with the head fully assembled, as it was removed from the engine. If oil consumption and/or oil smoke was an issue prior to the rebuild, you should have the head(s) disassembled to inspect and/or replace the valveguides, valveseals, or valveseats. This involves much more time and cost,

Cast-iron cylinder heads can be inspected for cracks using the Magnaflux method, similar to cylinder blocks. Cracks often form in or around the bolt holes and at the valveseats. The camshaft bearing caps' bearing bases on the head of an overhead-cam cylinder head should be carefully inspected for cracks, too. Because they are non-ferrous, aluminum heads typically require pressure testing when searching for cracks.

but it is essential to ensuring a tight, well-sealed engine that doesn't excessively consume oil. Some heads do not contain extremely durable valve guides or valveseats, which makes their replacement all the more critical.

Cylinder heads should be inspected for signs of warping and cracking, particularly aluminum heads. The heads absorb tremendous amounts of heat, and warping and cracking is not uncommon. Many engines are known to develop cracks or warping in specific areas. The machine shop should be aware of this and check the common damage areas. Warpage inspection can be accomplished by laying a straight edge diagonally across the deck-mounting surface. Gaps of 0.005 inch or more indicate a need for

machining. Even if no warping exists, the heads should at least be lightly machined or "surfaced" to promote a more accurate seal. Care must be taken to ensure too much material is not removed from the head because this could cause piston/valve clearance problems and/or affect the volume of the combustion chamber. Removing material from the head reduces chamber volume, effectively raising the engine's compression ratio. The ultimate result of this would be a detonation issue when the engine is assembled. The machine shop should check the manufacturer's specifications range before "cutting" the head(s). Heads that require severe machining may require lower-compression pistons and/or thicker head gaskets to maintain an acceptable compression ratio and piston-to-valve clearance. Overhead-cam cylinder heads, typically made of aluminum, are particularly prone to warping because aluminum is much softer than iron. Distortion is more prevalent toward the center of an aluminum head because thermal stress is the greatest in this area.

When it comes to checking for cracks, the machine shop should Magnaflux iron heads, similar to the process for inspecting the cylinder block. With aluminum heads, a pressure test is used. Minor cracks can generally be repaired on both iron and aluminum heads, but it is not uncommon to find cracked heads that are beyond repair capability. New or reconditioned heads are the only option in this case.

Valveseat, Valveguide and Valvestem Seal Repair and Replacement

As mentioned above, valveseat and valveguide repair and/or replacement should be considered on an engine that was burning or consuming oil prior to the rebuild. These non-moving components of the engine are subject to tremendous heat and can warp or wear to the

point of loosing their sealing properties. The valveseat is the large, round surface against which the valve heads seal, while the valveguides are the shafts in which the valvestems are "housed."

Many iron heads have integral valveseats that require machining, while others and aluminum heads have press-fit seats that can be cut out and replaced. Iron heads with integral seats can be machined to accept press-fit seats, which should be considered on engines built prior to approximately 1975 and the widespread implementation of unleaded fuel. By replacing original-style seats that were designed for leaded gasoline with contemporary hardened seats, the engine is able to use modern unleaded fuel without worry or the need for lead additives.

Valveseat machining and/or replacement should be accompanied by complementing machine work on the valve faces. They should be machined to match the angle of the new or machined valveseats. This

collective process is commonly referred to as a "valve job," and ensures a positive seal when the valves close.

Valveguides are capped with the valvestem seals and when either of these is worn, the telltale sign is usually a puff of blue oil smoke that occurs on a cold start. It happens when oil leaks past the stem seal and down the guide, pooling on the back of the valve face. It burns immediately when the engine is started. Reconditioning the valveguides can involve as little as reaming them within factory specifications or removing them and having new guides pressed into the head. With any luck, a cylinder head may only require the valvestem seals to be replaced, which will eliminate oil smoke in most cases.

A variety of materials are used on valveguides because their composition may require different actions to address reconditioning. Some guides are all steel, others are steel with bronze inserts, and others are full

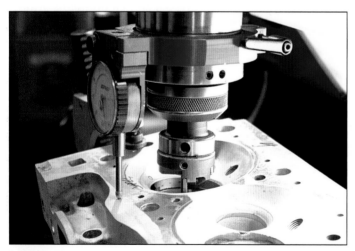

In this photo, a valveseat is being cut out of an aluminum cylinder head. It will be replaced with a new seat to help restore the valve's sealing. In fact, all of the head's seats will be replaced on this head. The area of the head beneath the seal may require machine work before the new seat is installed.

To match the angle of the new or machined valveseats, the valves are machined, too. Holding the valves at the desired angle and machining them with a high-speed cutting wheel accomplishes this. Increasing the number of angles on the valve head can improve airflow in and out of the engine, providing a slight increase in efficiency and/or performance. These changes must be matched with corresponding angle modifications to the valveseats.

bronze. Inserting new bronze inserts in steel guides is relatively easy, but every engine's requirements differ from the next.

From a budget perspective, replacing valvestem seals is significantly less expensive than valveseat and valveguide procedures because the stem seals can generally be

If a valveguide requires removal, an air-powered tool essentially "punches" the guide out of the head. Installing the new guide requires the same tool, but it punches the guide into the head from the opposite side.

replaced without the need for disassembling the cylinder head. Inspecting and repairing the valveseats and guides requires the heads to be

The cylinder head(s) require reassembly after the seats and/or guides are reconditioned. An air-powered valvespring compressor is the common tool for this job. The machine shop should offer this service if you don't have the facilities at your home garage to accomplish it. Hand-operated compressors can be rented from most auto parts stores if the builder intends to perform the head assembly at home.

removed. If oil consumption and blue smoke were *not* problems an engine suffered prior to the rebuilding process, installing new valvestem seals should be all that's required. Also, some engines are known for having seals that go bad, so inquiring with the machine shop may point to a blue smoke issue that can be cured with only replacement valveseals.

Balancing and Blueprinting: What Is It and Is It Necessary?

Typically mentioned in regard to high-performance engines, balancing and blueprinting are procedures used to maximize performance and reduce friction within an engine. What this means beyond the factory recommendations and guidelines for a rebuild process is: matching components so that there is little-to-no variances in weight (balancing); and tightening component tolerances (blueprinting). This process can include matching the weight of pistons, rods, and wrist pins,

Three styles of valveguides are seen here: on the left is a universal bronze insert, which is designed to be trimmed to length and inserted in a steel guide; in the middle is a steel guide that accepts the bronze insert; and on the right is a full bronze guide. The machine shop will provide guidance on the appropriate guide to use during the rebuild.

The machine shop technician inserts a gauge into the guides to determine whether the valveguides can be reused or require replacement. The measurement is taken against the size of the valvestems to determine the extent of wear.

or ensuring exactly matched combustion chamber volumes. These processes are effective at enhancing performance, but they are time consuming and generally not necessary for stock-type rebuilds.

Replacement and Reusable Engine Parts

A mail-order or auto-parts store-purchased rebuild kit is often the first thing rebuilders consider when they decide it's time to renew their engine. But it's important to wait before ordering the rebuild kit until the engine's cylinder block, crankshaft, and cylinder heads have been inspected. Machine work will likely require the use of plus-sized bearings and the like. Also, not every component on an engine requires replacement during the rebuilding process. Many parts, even critical reciprocating parts can be reused, as long as they pass a careful inspection.

Here's a look a the basic components and parts groups of an engine and what to do with them during the rebuild:

- Cylinder block: have it cleaned, machined, and inspected for cracks. If no cracks are found and the machine work falls within recommended specs, it's good to go.
- Freeze plugs/core plugs: replace all of them.
- Crankshaft: have it inspected, polished and, if necessary, "turned." It is reusable.
- Pistons: if the cylinder block requires *only* honing, the original pistons may be reused after they're inspected for cracks and/or excessive wear. If the cylinder block is over-bored, replacement oversized pistons *must* be used.

- Piston rings: get new rings. Do not reuse the originals.
- Connecting rods: reusable after inspection for cracks; crankshaft bores may require machining.
- Connecting rod bolts: reusable, but replace if the connecting rods also are replaced.
- Oil pump: new pump required (may also require pump drive shaft).
- Oil pan: clean it and reuse it.
- Camshaft: re-use depends on inspection for excessive wear on the journals and/or manufacturer directions. In most cases, a new camshaft will be required or should be used.
- Balance shafts (if equipped): reusable.
- Cylinder head: reusable after inspection and, generally, deck surfacing.
- Cylinder head bolts: replace

them. Some engines can reuse the originals, but it is cheap insurance to replace them with new bolts.
- Pushrods (if equipped): reusable.
- Valve lifters: reusable.
- Valvesprings and retainers: reusable, unless replacements are required with the use of a replacement camshaft with different-than-stock valve lift specifications.
- Timing chain/belt or camshaft drive chain/belt: replace on higher-mileage engines or those with unknown history; check for acceptable "play" on lower-mileage engines.
- Front cover/timing cover: reusable after inspection for warpage.
- Water pump: replace it. Do not reuse the original.
- Intake manifold: reusable after inspection for cracks.
- Exhaust manifolds and valve covers: reusable.

Here is a customer's complete machine-shop job, ready to be picked up and taken home for the assembly process. The block and heads have been machined, and new bearings were purchased to fit the various reconditioned bores.

- Harmonic balancer/damper: reusable.
- Spark plugs and wires: replace unless they were relatively new prior to the rebuild.
- Distributor: reusable, but the cap and rotor should be replaced along with the spark plugs and wires.
- Turbocharger: reusable, but it should be inspected for wear. High-mileage engines may require a rebuild or replacement.
- Supercharger: reusable, but should be inspected for wear.
- Carburetor: reusable, but may require cleaning or rebuilding.
- Throttle body: reusable after a thorough cleaning.
- Sensors, thermostat, etc.: replace if excessively corroded, recommended by the manufacturer, or they were problematic prior to the rebuild.
- Gaskets: replace all of them.

Miscellaneous external accessories, such as the serpentine belt, tensioner, and other engine-driven accessories, should be inspected prior to reuse and checked against the manufacturers' life expectancy specifications. It is often easier to replace the items and fit them while the engine is out of the car than do so after the engine is installed.

Carburetors: Renew, Rebuild or Replace?

A number of issues can be attributed to a "bad" carburetor: poor idling, stumbling or hesitation, inoperative choke, frequent flooding, etc., but it doesn't always mean a rebuild or replacement is required. Sometimes a thorough cleaning and inspection, as well as a replacement choke kit, may be all that's required to bring the carbure-

tor up to snuff. However, if it is clear the carburetor needs more detailed attention, rebuild kits are easy to find and inexpensive. Those with trepidation about building a carburetor can also send a carburetor to a rebuilding service or exchange it for a rebuilt model. Replacement should be the last option because it is the most costly.

A faulty or malfunctioning choke assembly that fails to open as the engine warms can cause a rough-running issue. This condition allows the carburetor to remain in a "rich" state during and after cold starts. The choke assembly can be inspected and repaired quickly and inexpensively. Lean conditions (too much air, not enough fuel) can cause stumbling, hesitation, and stalling. This may not always be sourced at the carburetor because the fuel line, fuel filter, and fuel pump could be the culprit.

Generally, a dirty, gummed-up carburetor can cause stalling, rough idling, and flooding. A thorough cleaning may help, but a rebuild is probably necessary. If you plan to attempt the job personally, precise information and identification numbers are required to obtain the correct rebuild kit. Sometimes the engine manufacturer, displacement, and model year are not sufficient. Often, identification tags are riveted to the carburetor and provide the information required for obtaining the precise kit.

At-Home Clean Up

While the cylinder block and other components are at the machine shop, you should inspect and clean the re-usable components of the engine. These include items

such as the intake manifold, accessory brackets, pulleys, etc. A parts washer with re-circulating solvent is the most effective method of cleaning these parts. Parts washers aren't common in many home garages, but they are becoming more affordable. For builders without access to a solvent-based parts washer, there are a number of parts-cleaning solutions that can be used to soak grimy parts. Brake cleaner and/or carburetor cleaner can be used to blast grime from smaller components and the corners of larger components. Gasket material should be scraped from every component, and care should be taken if doing this with an electric- or air-powered abrasive wheel because it can gouge some surfaces. In fact, many manufacturers advise against the use of high-power abrasive wheels and other tools.

While it is important for gasket surfaces to be clean and free of residue, the extent of cleaning on the rest of the engine's external components is up to you. Because a clean environment is essential to a quality engine assembly, the cleaner the parts, the easier the assembly process. Internal engine parts such as lifters and auxiliary/balance shafts shouldn't require much in the way of cleaning, unless a catastrophic engine failure caused debris to land on the parts. After the internal parts have been removed and inspected, they can be set aside and covered to prevent them from becoming unnecessarily dirty.

Painting

In addition to simple cleaning, a coat or two of paint will provide important protection for many components. In addition to corrosion

A parts cleaner is the easiest way to scrub accumulated grime off engine parts. For builders without access to one in their home shop, old-fashioned elbow grease and cans of brake cleaner, lacquer thinner, and other solvents will get the job done.

Whenever possible, use a scraper to get rid of gasket residue and other debris. It is faster and easier to use an air-powered grinder or scuffing tool, but being too aggressive use can gall surfaces, particularly the softer material of aluminum parts.

protection, paint often makes a part look like new by enhancing the fresh look of the rebuilt engine, and it is accomplished with simple spray paint. Pulleys, brackets, and valve covers can all be restored to like-new condition with paint. Even cast-iron exhaust manifolds can be renewed with high-temperature paint or brush-on coating (see accompanying photos). The heat generated by the engine and exhaust system requires specific paint for different components, but generally speaking, high-temperature engine-specific paint should be used on the cylinder block, cylinder heads, water pump, intake manifold, and other cast-iron components. Very high-temperature paint or coatings should be used on exhaust manifolds. Use either color-matching conventional paint or high-temp engine paint for other components, such accessory brackets and pulleys. High-temperature paint typically requires a curing period of

12 to 24 hours, so you should plan to paint the cylinder block and other components at least a day before the final assembly begins.

When it comes to painting the cylinder block and heads, care should be taken to prevent paint from spraying onto gasket surfaces, bearing journals, cylinder bores, the

Engine paint comes in a variety of temperature-scaled formulas. The very high-temperature paint on the left is for exhaust manifolds, while the high-temperature paint on the right can be used on most other iron and steel engine components.

heads' deck surfaces, and the valve-train area. Taping off these areas is the easiest method to prevent over-spray from reaching them.

Here's an example of engine painting, showing the block, heads, oil pan, and valve covers sprayed with the same color. Note the installed old spark plugs and taped-over exhaust ports, which prevent the paint from spraying where it shouldn't. The oil filter even receives overspray, but that's OK because the engine will receive its first oil and filter change within the first 300 miles, or so.

SHORT BLOCK ASSEMBLY

Tools and Materials Required

- Engine stand
- Torque wrench and/or torque angle meter
- Sockets, including deep-wells
- Wrenches
- Screwdrivers/nut drivers
- Feeler gauge and/or dial-pointer instrument
- Piston ring compressor/piston installation tool
- Engine assembly lube
- Camshaft /lifter lube (if required)
- RTV-type (or equivalent) sealer
- Thread sealant
- Plastigage

Engine assembly begins when the machine shop has finished with the cylinder block and other components. You should have the remaining engine parts cleaned, prepped, and ready for installation. The new components for the engine, such as gaskets, fasteners, camshaft, etc., should also be procured. Use the recommended sizes for bearings, pistons, etc., as determined by the machine shop work. For most engines, very complete rebuild kits (often called master kits) are available, and they can be ordered with the plus-sized bearings, pistons, and other components. These kits are generally more cost-effective than sourcing the parts individually, and they are available through most auto parts stores and online parts sources, such as rock-auto.com. For engines that don't require new pistons or a camshaft, partial kits are available and include a complete gasket set and other necessary parts. Camshafts are typically *not* included with overhead-cam engine master kits. In many cases, the cams from these engines are reusable. In those cases where they need to be replaced, they'll have to be sourced separately from the master rebuild kit.

Master kits typically include the following:

- Gaskets
- Freeze/core plugs
- Main bearings
- Rod bearings
- Pistons and rings
- Timing belt/chain
- Oil pump
- Camshaft (cam-in-block engines)
- Lifters (cam-in-block engines)

Depending on the engine, some master kits include thrust washers, rod bushings, and other incidental components. Engines with over-bored cylinders require larger-diameter pistons and rings, and even if the original pistons are re-used, they must be fitted with new rings. A machined crankshaft requires oversized main bearings and/or rod bearings. Typically, these components are ordered in several common "plus" sizes, including 0.020 inch (0.50 mm), 0.030 inch (0.75 mm), or 0.040 inch (1 mm) for the pistons and rings; and 0.010 inch (0.25 mm), 0.020 inch (0.50 mm), or 0.030 inch (0.75 mm) for the main and rod bearings. The machine shop will provide the specifications required to order a master kit with the correctly sized components.

Prices vary greatly on rebuild kits, with some offering upgrades to premium materials and components. Premium gaskets and fasteners are wise investments, but for a stock-type rebuild, there is no reason to upgrade from a cast (also known as hypereutectic) piston to forged aluminum. The manufacturer's recommendations and original-style material should be used.

Engine assembly kits include the gaskets, bearings, and other new components needed during the build procedure. The machining process determines the size of the bearings, pistons, and other components that need to be ordered.

Pistons are typically included in master rebuild kits, but you must specify the size, based on whether the cylinders were overbored at the machine shop. When delivered, they should be inspected for damage, such as cracks, that may have originated during shipping. With new pistons, matching them to a specific cylinder isn't necessary, but when re-using the original pistons, they must be used within the original cylinders.

A new camshaft is generally included in master kits for pushrod engines, but not overhead-cam engines. The distributor gear section should be cleaned with mineral spirits, carburetor cleaner, or even a light wire brush prior to installation.

When ordering a master kit, you must specify whether it requires plus-sized main bearings and/or rod bearings, based on machine work performed on the crankshaft.

Engine assembly lubrication is essential. It is available through all auto parts sources and should be used instead of motor oil for most assembly procedures. The high-viscosity lube clings longer to parts, ensuring sufficient lubrication during the time-consuming procedures of building the engine, installing it, and preparing it for start-up.

Engine assembly lubricant, gasket sealer, and motor oil are required for the short-block assembly. Engine assembly lube is "thicker" than standard motor oil and holds onto the parts longer than motor oil. This gives the components, particularly the camshaft and various bearings, an extra measure of protection that is important during the start-up and break-in procedures. For that reason, I do not recommend assembling the engine with only motor oil as a lubricant. Assembly lube should be used on rocker arm fulcrum balls, needle bearings, rocker arm roller tips or rocker shafts, timing chain sprockets/gears, roller lifters and camshafts, and bearing surfaces. In addition, some camshafts and lifters, typically solid-lifter-type cams, require dedicated camshaft lubricant that is brushed on in a paste-like form. You should check the factory service manual for camshaft lubricant requirements.

Also, if the block uses dowels to locate the cylinder heads, main bearings, or other components, they should be installed prior to the assembly process. Often, these are installed by the machine shop, but if not, they can be easily installed by simply tapping them into the appropriate holes with a mallet.

General Information

The photos in this chapter primarily depict the assembly of the Ford 4-cylinder engine seen in previous chapters. It is an inline-type overhead-cam engine that is assembled with the basic procedures used on most automotive engines. That said, the assembly photos and descriptions contained in this chapter focus on general assembly procedures; it is not necessarily a step-by-step guide for building a Ford 2.3-liter engine. Builders of cam-in-block engines should see the special section, "Building the Cam-in-Block Rotating Assembly," in this chapter before starting their own engine build because the assembly procedures involving the overhead-cam configuration differ significantly from those involving the camshaft and timing gear of a cam-in-block (pushrod) engine.

Regardless of the engine type, you should approach the short-block assembly project with patience and attention to detail. Rushing the project and skipping inspection procedures, for example, usually produces an imprecise engine that will likely be down on power and longevity. A very clean, well-lit build area is a must, too.

Preparing the Cylinder Block

Prior to installing the first component on the engine, the cylinder block must be thoroughly cleaned, even after it comes back washed from the machine shop. A lint-free cloth or tack cloth sprayed with carburetor cleaner is preferred, particularly for the cylinder bores. The engine should be free of dirt, dust, and oil. If you have an air compressor, the block should be blown clean, with air blown through all of the bolt holes, coolant passages, and other crevices. If the cylinder block requires painting, it can be done relatively quickly and easily with spray cans. The cylinder deck(s) and the bottom of the block should be taped off. You should avoid paint overspray from landing on bearing surfaces, the cylinder deck, and the cylinder bores. When the block is cleaned and painted, the short-block assembly can begin.

Checking Bearing Clearances

During the assembly process, it is important to check the bearing clearance—the space between the bearing and journal that is separated by oil—of items such as the crankshaft and connecting rods. This is typically done with a plastic, oil-soluble material known by its trade name, Plastigage. The tool is essentially a thin strip of plastic material that is laid upon the bearing surface. The crankshaft or connecting rod is then installed to the factory specification and removed again. The Plastigage flattens against the journal as the bearing cap is torqued down. The width of flattened Plastigage is measured in thousandths of an inch (a scale is included on the packaging), determining whether the bearing clearance is within factory specifications.

Because there are several sizes of Plastigage—MPG-1 (green), MPR-1 (red), MPB-1 (blue), and MPY-1 (yellow)—you should check the factory bearing specs prior to purchasing the tool, so that Plastigage with the correct measurable range is obtained.

For space considerations, the rod bearing installation procedure is demonstrated in this chapter, although the procedure should be employed on the crankshaft/main bearing clearances, too. There are other components that may require clearance checks that are performed with Plastigage; the factory service manual should call out these instances.

A Note About Mechanical Fuel Pump Installation

An installation procedure not covered in the photos of this chapter is the mechanical fuel pump of older-style carbureted engines. I omitted this step for space reasons, and cite the widespread use of fuel injection on production engines of the last 25 years. These engines typically use high-pressure, inline or in-tank fuel pumps (or both), similar to the 4-cylinder engine depicted throughout this book. Builders with an engine using a block-mounted mechanical fuel pump should reference the factory service manual for the proper installation procedure.

Cast or Forged: Should You Upgrade?

When talk of engine performance and strength comes up, it invariably leads to the debate of cast versus forged components. Except on some higher-end, high-performance, and turbocharged or supercharged examples, most factory-built engines are equipped with cast components. This includes the pistons and crankshaft; the pistons are typically cast with a hypereutectic alloy while the crankshaft is cast steel. Older-style connecting rods are usually steel, while later-model engines typically use connecting rods made from powdered metal that is formed under tremendous pressure.

Forged crankshafts, pistons, and rods are essentially pounded or pressed into shape. Such parts are generally considered stronger, more durable, and better at withstanding high-load or high-performance operation. Many engine builders feel the urge to upgrade their factory cast components with stronger forged parts, but, unless you are assembling an engine with considerably higher power output than stock, this is an unnecessary and costly investment.

Modern cast replacement parts are very strong and for the builder who is building an engine more or less to factory specifications, they are more than sufficiently strong and durable. Indeed, even many high-performance production cars, such as the Chevrolet Corvette, use hypereutectic pistons. And while there is no denying the durability properties of forged parts, they have their drawbacks on a stock-type rebuild. For one thing, forged pistons do not expand with heat nearly as much as hypereutectic pistons. This can lead to a knocking-type or rattling noise when the engine is cold-started and even when it is warmed up, caused by the pistons physically knocking against the cylinder walls. Also, building to stock specs with forged rotating parts, such as the pistons and crankshaft, can actually negatively affect performance because forged components are typically heavier than cast parts. With everything else being stock, this could affect the engine's ability to rev quickly and such a setup could sap horsepower as more of it is required to turn the heavier components. An otherwise-stock engine simply wasn't designed to use the heavier forged parts.

For high-performance engine builds, forged parts should be considered, but for stock-type rebuilds, there's no need to spend the extra money. The cast parts will hold up fine and deliver quiet, dependable performance.

1 Ready to Assemble

The Ford cylinder block is back from the machine shop, installed on the engine stand, and ready for the engine assembly to begin. The main bearing caps were installed at delivery because the block was align-honed, but they must be removed before the assembly commences. Although it doesn't look like it, the block was painted an industrial gray, matching the factory finish.

2 Clean the Block

Wiping down and cleaning the block after it returns from the machine shop is a must. The engine, particularly the cylinder bores, should be free of dirt, debris, and oil. If possible, the block should be blown clean with compressed air, including all of the bolt holes and coolant passages.

3 Install Freeze Plugs

If the freeze plugs were not installed at the machine shop, you should install them first. The plugs need to be driven straight into the block using a mallet or hammer and a socket as wide as the inner diameter of the plug. No sealant or lubricant is used with this task, but you must strike the plug accurately and confidently to avoid bending the plug or driving it in unevenly. In many cases, the plugs will "bottom out" in the block, indicating they're seated.

4 Install Main Bearings

After the block's main journals have been wiped clean, the main bearings are installed. Many builders start at the center with the thrust bearing because the larger bearing has "wings." The main bearings are installed dry with no lubricant or sealant. They simply snap into place when pressed onto the journal.

The main bearings typically have slots that correspond with oiling holes located in the main journals. It is important to double check that each main journal with an oiling hole is matched with a bearing that has a corresponding oil slot.

5 Lubricate Main Bearings

After installation, treat the main bearings with engine assembly lube in preparation for the crankshaft's installation. Only a couple of drops are necessary. Use a finger to spread the lubricant all over the bearing surface.

Important!

6 Install Crankshaft (Overhead-Cam Engines)

The crankshaft should be wiped clean prior to installation and carefully lowered onto the main bearings. Once it is in place, the crankshaft should be rotated a few times by hand to spread the lube all over the crankshaft journals and ensure there are no rotation impediments or hang-ups. NOTE: Some crankshafts use a press-fit timing sprocket that must be installed prior to the crankshaft's installation in the engine.

Professional Mechanic Tip

7 Install and Lubricate Main Bearing Caps

Similar to the procedure for the main bearing journals on the block, the main cap journals require bearings that snap into place. Prior to installation, they should be lubricated with engine assembly lube. Although it doesn't happen often, you may find bearings that don't exactly line up with the slots in the bearing cap. If this is the case, the tangs on the bearings can be filed down to fit. If that doesn't work, the build procedure must halt while new bearings are located.

8 Install Main Bearing Caps

The main bearing caps should be carefully installed by hand, and a rubber mallet or dead-blow hammer may be needed to seat them accurately on the block. A light coat of motor oil or engine lube can be used on the bolt threads, but only a light coat. If oil pools at the bottom of the bolt hole, it may cause problems during the bolt-torque procedure. At this stage, the caps should be only snugged down and not yet final-torqued. NOTE: It may be necessary on some engines to install the rear oil seal during this time. Check the manufacturer's recommendation.

9 Rotate the Crankshaft

With the main caps snugged in place, the crankshaft should rotate freely. If it does not rotate easily or is locked in place, pull off the main caps and repeat the procedure. Pull off one cap at a time and rotate the crankshaft to check whether a single cap and/or its bearing is the cause of the problem. If this does not provide the answer and the problem persists, do not proceed with the engine build until it is resolved. It is likely the builder will have to consult with a professional and return the block, crank, and bearing caps to the machine shop for additional work.

REBUILDING ANY AUTOMOTIVE ENGINE

Professional Mechanic Tip, Torque Fasteners

10 Prepare for Final Main Cap Tightening Sequence

  The main caps are tightened to a specification determined by the engine manufacturer. In many cases, it is advantageous to set the torque wrench to a lower specification, such as 50 ft-lbs, and pre-tighten the caps to this consistent spec. It sets up the block for more even pressure when the caps are fastened to the final factory specification.

Torque Fasteners, Important!

11 Follow the Factory Manual for Torque Specs and Sequences

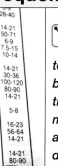

BELT BOLT)		38-54	28-40
CAMSHAFT GEAR BOLT	M-8	19-28	14-21
CAMSHAFT THRUST PLATE BOLT	M-12	68-96	50-71
CARBURETOR TO SPACER STUD	M-6	8-12	6-9
CARBURETOR TO SPACER NUT	M-8	10-20	7.5-15
CARBURETOR SPACER — TO MANIFOLD BOLT	M-8	14-19	10-14
CONNECTING ROD NUT ⑪	M-8	19-28	14-21
CRANKSHAFT DAMPER BOLT	M-9	41-49	30-36
CYLINDER HEAD BOLT ⑫	M-14	136-162	100-120
DISTRIBUTOR CLAMP BOLT	M-12	108-122	80-90
DISTRIBUTOR VACUUM TUBE TO MANIFOLD ADAPTER	M-10	19-28	14-21
EXHAUST MANIFOLD TO CYLINDER HEAD BOLT, STUD OR NUT ⑬		7-11	5-8
FLYWHEEL TO CRANKCASE BOLT	M-10	22-31	16-23
FUEL PUMP TO CYLINDER BLOCK	M-10	73-87	56-64
INTAKE MANIFOLD TO CYLINDER HEAD BOLT NUT —	M-8	19-28	14-21
MAIN BEARING CAP BOLT ⑮	M-8	19-28	14-21
OIL PRESSURE SENDING WIRE TO BLOCK	M-12	108-122	80-90
OIL PUMP PICKUP TUBE TO PUMP			
NUT TURBO TO MANIFOLD	M-18	11-2	
NUT, OIL SUPPLY LINE		19	
NUT, OIL SUPPLY LINE FITTING		38	
BOLT, OIL RETURN TO TURBO		27	
NUT, OIL RETURN TO FITTING		12-1	
NUT, OIL RETURN FITTING TO UPPER BLOCK		19-2 12-16	

  Each engine has specific fastener torque specifications that must be referenced before the final tightening procedure. The manufacturer may also require a two- or three-stage procedure, as well as a specific torque sequence. The multi-stage sequence is typical of later-model engines that use torque-to-yield fasteners.

Precision Measurement, Torque Fasteners

12 Torque Main Caps

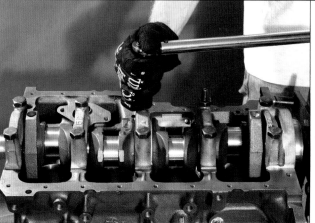

Generally, main caps are torqued starting with the center cap and working outward in a clockwise spiral pattern. That means the cap to the right of the center cap would be torqued next; with the cap to the left of the center cap after that and so on. The crankshaft-to-main bearing clearance should be checked at this point. See the photos and captions later in this chapter or the main text earlier for a description of the procedure.

Important! Precision Measurement

13 Check Crankshaft Endplay

Acceptable crankshaft endplay (the amount of thrust or "walking" a crankshaft will do in the cylinder block) is generally between 0.004 and 0.006 inch. To check, insert a feeler gauge between the bearing and crankshaft, or use a dial-pointer gauge that is placed at the front of the crankshaft (seen here). A screwdriver is used to push the crankshaft forward and aft in the block, with the pointer providing a readout on the dial gauge, indicating whether the thrust is within the acceptable range. Checking endplay is important because an excessive amount of endplay will prematurely wear the main bearings. If there is excessive endplay, installing a thicker thrust bearing usually solves the problem. If that doesn't fix the problem, the builder will likely have to return the block and crankshaft to the machine shop.

14 Prepare to Install Rod/Piston Assemblies (All Engines)

Assuming the rods and pistons are pre-assembled, the piston rings must be installed, but not before they are checked in the cylinder bores for an acceptable end-gap specification. The piston rings are then installed on the pistons. They typically include a pair of compression rings and a lower, multi-layer oil control ring.

15 Check Piston Ring End Gap

For each piston, insert the ring into the cylinder bore and check the gap with a feeler gauge to verify the ring end gap. Note the small, round indent on the piston ring; it indicates the top side.

After the ring is placed inside the cylinder bore, the top of the piston is used to square the ring within the bore, providing a more accurate, as-installed position of the ring for the feeler gauge. The ring should be located approximately 1/2 inch down in the cylinder bore.

Precision Measurement, Important!

16 Measure Piston Ring End Gap

The feeler gauge is inserted in the small gap between the ends of the piston ring in the cylinder bore. Some file-to-fit-type rings can be modified to fit within the manufacturer's gap specifications, but non-file rings that don't fit within the specification range must be replaced.

17 Install Piston Rings

Special Tool

With the end gap specs confirmed, the piston rings can be installed on the pistons. It is a tight fit, but the rings simply wrap around the piston head and snap into the appropriate ring land (groove). The installation order should be as follows: bottom ring land—lower oil control ring, oil expansion ring (the corrugated ring), upper oil control ring; center ring land—lower compression ring; and, top ring land—upper compression ring.

18 Correct Ring Position

Professional Mechanic Tip, Important!

In addition to ensuring the correct position for the compression rings, the rings must also be installed with the top side facing up. The top is usually marked similar to the indented indicator seen on this ring. Also, many professional builders adjust the rings so that none of the end gaps are lined up with one another. The idea is to prevent a direct path for oil, avoiding blow-by or reduced compression.

19 Install Connecting Rod Bearings

After the piston rings are installed, the pistons are turned over, the bearings are installed on the connecting rods, and the connecting rod caps are snugged down. They snap into place without any assembly lube, but the bearing faces should be coated with lube prior to installation in the engine.

20 Clean Cylinder Bores

With the rod bearings installed, the piston assemblies are ready for installation, but the cylinder bores should be wiped clean one more time, prior to installing the rods and pistons. Brake or carburetor cleaner (or similar) sprayed on a lint-free rag does the trick.

Special Tool, Important!

21 Install Rod/Piston Assemblies

Using a piston ring compressor or similar tool, the rod/piston assembly is slipped into the cylinder bore. Typically, an indication mark on the top of the piston points toward the front of the engine. Extreme care must be taken to prevent scratching, dinging, or other damage to the bores as the assembly is installed. Slipping small pieces of vacuum hose over the connecting rod studs helps prevent scratching. NOTE: You should make sure to double-check that each assembly is matched with the correct cylinder bore, if required. On most production-spec rebuilds that use new pistons, it is probably not necessary to match the piston and cylinder bores, but high-performance, blueprinted engines (see Chapter 4) with very specific tolerances require piston/bore matching.

The handle end of a mallet is often required to tap the piston assembly down into the bore, particularly after the rings have expanded within the walls. The assembly is pushed down until the rod end meets the crankshaft journal. At this point, a light touch is necessary and nothing should be forced. If the piston/rod assembly doesn't slide relatively easily down through the bore, it should be removed and inspected.

22 Install Rod Caps

When the connecting rod is seated on the crankshaft journal, a lubricated rod cap is slipped on and snugged down. It is not necessary to final-torque the cap at this point because the rotating assembly must first be checked for rotational impediments.

The crankshaft should be turned with a breaker bar after each rod is installed to ensure unimpeded rotation. The friction of all the piston rings within the cylinders makes turning the rotating assembly by hand all but impossible.

Torque Fasteners

23 Torque Rod Caps

 Similar to the main bearing caps, the rod caps are torqued to factory specifications; however, there is generally no center-out sequence required; they are torqued one cap at a time.

Precision Measurement

24 Check Rod Bearing Clearance

When the con- necting rods are fastened, they should be checked for in- spec bearing clear- ance. This is done by removing the caps and using a crushable tool called Plastigage.

Torque Fasteners, Special Tool

25 Torque Rod Caps

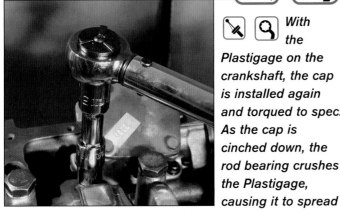

 With the Plastigage on the crankshaft, the cap is installed again and torqued to spec. As the cap is cinched down, the rod bearing crushes the Plastigage, causing it to spread out on the crankshaft journal. The width of the crushed gauge material determines the clearance between the bearing and journal as oil circulates through the engine.

After the rod cap is removed, a small piece of Plastigage is placed on the crankshaft journal, spanning the width of the journal. There are different sizes of Plastigage that are identified by color. Therefore, you should consult the service manual for the specification and purchase the size that fits the range indicated by the manual.

Precision Measurement

26 Measure Rod Bearing Clearance

After the cap is torqued, it is again removed and the crushed area of the Plastigage material is measured (the Plastigage package includes the appropriate gauge). If the width of the crushed material falls within factory specifi- cations, the bearing clearance is good. In the case of the engine seen here, the crush material measured 0.0015 inch, which was within the range of acceptability. NOTE: This method of clearance testing can be applied to many other engine components, such as the main bearings. The author chose to focus on the rod bearings for this book because their specification is vitally important to engine longevity.

Torque Fasteners, Important!

27 Re-Install Rod Caps and Re-Torque

 With the rod bearing clearances checked and confirmed, the rod caps are re-installed and torqued again to factory specifications. When all of the connecting rods have been installed, all bearing clearances are confirmed and re-torqued to spec, the rotating assembly is completed. The assembly should be rotated again with the breaker bar to double-check that there are no hang-ups.

28 Install Oil Pump

A new oil pump should be used on a rebuilt engine, which typically requires it to be mounted to the pick-up tube. On this engine, they are installed as a single assembly. Some new oil pumps come with a new pick-up, but many do not. It is important, then, to ensure that the re-used pick-up is clean and free of sludge, debris, or other foreign matter that could impede oil flow.

Important!

29 Prime Oil Pump

Filling the oil pump pick-up with motor oil primes the oil pump for the start-up procedure. This is especially important for engines with oiling systems that cannot be easily primed at the start-up stage, such as some overhead-cam engines and engines with distributorless ignition systems.

Torque Fasteners

31 Install Front Cover

With the seal installed on the front cover, the cover is then bolted to the front of the cylinder block. Like other important parts of the rotating assembly, it has a fastener torque spec that must be followed exactly. Too little or too much torque may enable an oil leak.

30 Install Front Oil Seal

On many engines, the front oil seal is mounted to a cover that slips over the front hub of the crankshaft and may or may not cover the timing chain/belt. If the seal is mounted on the front cover (as seen here), the seal must be pressed on to the cover; typically, the installation requires careful yet forceful application of a mallet. If the mallet end isn't a close match to the seal's diameter, a socket or similar tool can be used. Care must be taken to avoid bending the edges of the delicate seal because any damage renders the seal unusable.

32 Install Auxiliary or Balance Shafts

This four-cylinder engine is equipped with an auxiliary shaft that will be connected to a sprocket to drive the distributor. Other engines use a similarly designed balance shaft (typically found only on inline-type engines) that is also installed after the front cover. A thrust plate keeps the shaft in place.

Professional Mechanic Tip PRO TIP

35 Install Oil Pan

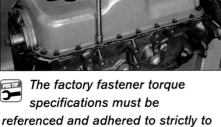

PRO TIP The factory fastener torque specifications must be referenced and adhered to strictly to prevent leaks. Over-tightening the oil pan can crush or deform the gasket, causing a leak path. Also, the center-out, spiral method is recommended for cinching the fasteners. The builder should proceed in stages, going over the fasteners repeatedly to ensure even pressure during the tightening sequence. It is typically a lengthy process to ensure accurate fastening.

33 Install Water Pump

Another all-new part to be installed is the water pump. Make sure the correct water pump gasket is used because manufacturers often have different water pump applications for the same basic engine family. The installation of an incorrect gasket could lead to coolant leakage at start-up. RTV-type sealant is used around the gasket and pump to help prevent leaks.

34 Prepare to Install Oil Pan

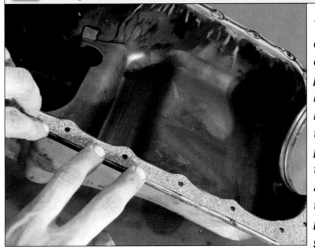

The method varies, depending on the type of oil pan and gasket, but preparing the oil pan for installation involves running a bead of RTV-type sealant along the oil pan mounting flange, or the corresponding rail around the perimeter of the engine block, and pressing on the oil pan gasket. Only a light bead of sealant is required; too much will spill over when the pan is tightened. Some later-model engines use O-ring-type seals that do not require sealant.

36 Prepare to Install Valve Lifters (Cam-in-Block Engines Only)

After the oil pan is installed, the engine can be turned upright in order to install the valve lifters. Hydraulic-type lifters should be soaked in or doused with motor oil prior to installation. As seen here, a cup filled with motor oil and the lifters are thoroughly immersed in it prior to installation. Solid lifters need only to be lubricated with motor oil or assembly lube as they're being installed.

37 Install Lifter Retainers (If Equipped)

On engines equipped with lifter retaining devices, they are installed after the lifters have been slipped into their bores.

The retainers on the cam-in-block engine in the previous three photos use a "spider"-type tray to hold the lifter retainers in place. Its "arms" hold down the retainers after the tray is torqued to spec.

38 Install Crankshaft Sprocket

At this stage of the short block's assembly, the crankshaft sprocket on a pushrod-type engine or a crankshaft with a press-fit sprocket should be installed if it hasn't been done already. With this type of engine, the sprocket simply aligns with the keyway and slips onto the crankshaft hub. Thread locking compound should be used on the fastener.

39 Install Auxiliary Shaft Sprocket (If Equipped)

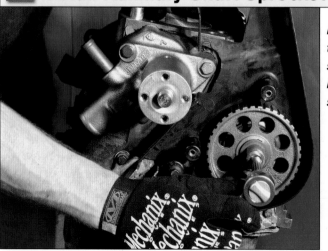

For engines equipped with auxiliary shafts or balance shafts, the drive sprocket is installed along with the crankshaft sprocket. On this engine, a backing cover for the timing belt has also been installed. Like the crankshaft sprocket, thread sealant should be used on the fastening bolts.

40 Install Block-Mounted Sensors

Temperature, knock and/or oil pressure sensors, sending units, or switches should be installed on the cylinder block as the short-block assembly draws to a close. If a Teflon-based thread sealer is used, do not use Teflon tape; use only the brush-on paste-type. This is particularly important for any sensor that intrudes on a coolant passage because tape sealant could break off in the water jacket, fouling a coolant passage.

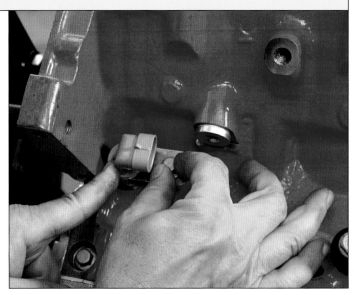

Engines equipped with a crank-triggered ignition system rather than a conventional distributor require additional block-mounted sensors, including crankshaft position and camshaft position sensors. They should be installed during the short-block assembly. Here, the crankshaft position sensor is installed on a GM LS V-8 engine.

Important!

41 Install Miscellaneous Block-Mounted Components

Because all engines are different, each has features that are not found on other engines. In the case of this turbocharged Ford engine, a block-mounted oil cooler is part of the short-block assembly. Rely on reference photos taken during disassembly to ensure the correct mounting location and orientation of the part.

42 Final Short-Block Assembly

With the "bottom end" of the engine completed, attention will turn to installing the cylinder head and the remainder of engine components.

Building the Cam-in-Block Rotating Assembly

The builder of a pushrod engine has a different procedure than the builder of an overhead-cam engine. It begins with the installation of the camshaft (and, if necessary, a retainer or thrust plate) and is followed by the installation of the crankshaft and timing set. This sets up the rotating assembly and positions the camshaft and crankshaft in the correct relationship with one another. With this rotating assembly completed, the remainder of the short block assembly generally follows the steps outlined previously in this chapter.

Similar to the procedure for checking crankshaft end play, including a dial indicator and/or feeler gauge, camshaft end play should be checked after installation, primarily on engines with roller lifter valvetrains (hydraulic- or solid-type). A small amount of end play, generally between 0.005 and 0.010 inch, is necessary on roller-type camshafts to prevent wear occurring as a result of interference between the camshaft and other engine parts.

Checking end play is not required of engines that use a non-roller hydraulic or flat-tappet camshaft; also, engines that use a thrust plate or camshaft retaining plate do not require the end play to be checked. Note that the procedures outlined in this section depict the major steps. You should consult the rest of the chapter for information on bearing installation, camshaft lubricant, etc.

Camshaft Installation (Cam-in-Block Engines). With a pushrod engine, many professional engine builders start the assembly process by installing a lubricated camshaft, which is carefully inserted into the cylinder block to avoid damaging the camshaft bearings. Camshaft installation tools ease the process, but threading a long bolt into one of the holes for the timing gear sprocket works, too.

Next, the main caps are tightened to the factory specifications. Again, see the photos and captions earlier in this section for a complete description of the procedure.

After the camshaft comes the crankshaft. It is set in place with the same procedures outlined earlier in this chapter.

The timing sprocket is pushed onto the crankshaft hub, with the round position indicator pointed toward the camshaft.

Filling the oil pump pick-up with motor oil primes the oil pump for the start-up procedure. This is especially important for engines with oiling systems that cannot be easily primed at the start-up stage, such as some overhead-cam engines and engines with distributorless ignition systems.

Degreeing the Camshaft: Is it Necessary?

Degreeing is the method that ensures the camshaft is perfectly aligned for accurate timing—more so than simply relying on alignment marks on the timing gears. Machining of the crankshaft can result in variances that can affect camshaft alignment. Generally, the method involves using a large degree wheel and a block-mounted pointer to determine the maximum camshaft lift on lobe number-1 with top dead center on cylinder number-1. This is called the centerline method and is the easiest way of degreeing a camshaft.

Although rebuilt engines are likely to receive several machining procedures, if they are rebuilt to stock specifications, the slight variances should not drastically affect camshaft timing. Similarly, a replacement camshaft with stock lift and duration specs should line up accurately without the need for degreeing.

For balanced and blueprinted engines and high-performance rebuilds with non-stock camshaft specs, degreeing provides an extra measure of accuracy. But for the vast majority of stock-type rebuilds, degreeing is unnecessary.

We don't recommend camshaft degreeing for stock-type engine rebuilds. Stock-spec camshafts should provide accurate timing when installed with the correct relationship to the crankshaft.

FINAL ENGINE ASSEMBLY

Tools and Materials Required

- Torque wrench and/or torque angle meter
- Sockets, including deep-wells
- Breaker bar
- Wrenches
- Screwdrivers/nut drivers
- Engine assembly lube
- RTV-type (or equivalent) sealer
- Thread sealant

The short-block assembly comprised the bulk of component installation on the engine, but the final assembly steps—including the installation of the cylinder head(s) and distributor—are vitally important to ensuring the engine starts, runs, and performs as desired. This chapter outlines the basic procedures for finalizing the engine assembly for both cam-in-block and overhead-cam engines. The primary difference in these assembly steps includes: the installation of the timing gear on the Ford overhead-cam engine depicted throughout this book, as the timing gear was installed as part of the short-block assembly (Chapter 5) on

a cam-in-block engine, and the pushrod and rocker arm assemblies for cam-in-block engines, which require assembly steps not applicable to the overhead-cam engine. This chapter also proceeds with the assumption that the builder is

installing pre-assembled cylinder heads. For overhead-cam engines, this means the valves, springs, rocker arms, and the camshaft. For cam-in-block engines, the complete head assembly includes the valves and valvesprings (including retainers).

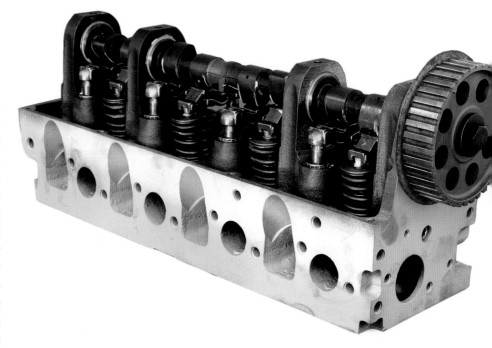

This chapter details the engine assembly process using pre-assembled cylinder heads. In the case of the Ford overhead-cam engine depicted throughout this book, the head was rebuilt with a new camshaft and new valveseals, along with light machining of the deck-mounting surface.

Cylinder Head Bolt Considerations

The service manual of some engines advise to reuse the cylinder head bolts during the engine assembly if it is permissible. However, I suggest investing in brand-new head bolts. Imperceptible stretching of the original bolts typically renders them undesirable, even if the manufacturer suggests they are re-usable. This is a tip that should be especially followed by builders who started with an engine that was subjected to prolonged or severe overheating.

Head bolts are designed to stretch, if ever so slightly. This allows the head bolts to exert force upon components' surfaces, binding them together. Stretching also takes into account the crushability of the gasket between the head and cylinder block, allowing for an optimized seal. In short, the stretch capability of the bolt gives it its clamping power. When tightened to its final, factory-torque specification, a head bolt may stretch up to 0.010 inch. Additional stretching occurs as the engine heats up, with the head bolts in aluminum heads typically subjected to more heat and stretching than those in cast iron heads.

The question of head bolt re-use is irrelevant to engines built with torque-to-yield (TTY) fasteners, which is true of many later-model engines. TTY head bolts are designed to stretch significantly during installation to provide exceptional clamping power and, as such, can be installed only one time—at the time of the original assembly. Once they are removed, they *must* be replaced with new fasteners. Also, a conventional torque wrench cannot be used with TTY fasteners; they must be tightened with a torque angle meter. TTY bolts are typically longer, thinner, and lighter in color than conventional head bolts. If you are unsure whether your engine uses TTY fasteners or not, a quick check in the service manual or at an online source should provide immediate confirmation.

When it comes to installing head bolts, a light coat of motor oil is recommended for the threads; this reduces friction and multiplies the clamping power of the bolt at a given torque specification. Too much oil on the bolt can cause a hydrolock condition in "blind" (head bolts that do not protrude into a water jacket) head bolt holes. That is, too much oil in the holes puts too much pressure on the bolt prior to it being tightened to the final torque specification. The result could be an inaccurately fastened bolt or bolt failure. Similar problems can arise if old, dirty bolts are reused; the grime on the threads can cause false torque readings. Bolts that protrude into a water jacket should be coated in a sealer to prevent coolant leaks.

Cylinder head bolts for aluminum heads are typically used with flat washers to prevent the hardened bolt head from galling or digging into the softer aluminum material of the head. You should install the washers with the bolts during the assembly process.

Bottom line: Head bolts are relatively inexpensive—anywhere from $20 to $40 a set, in most cases—and represent cheap insurance against future engine problems.

Pushrods, Rocker Arms and Other Valvetrain Checks

As previously mentioned, the biggest difference between the final assembly procedures of a cam-in-block (pushrod) engine and an overhead-cam engine are the steps required to install pushrods and rocker arms on the cam-in-block engine. This occurs after the cylinder heads have been installed. The pushrods can be reused if they are found to be straight and undamaged. The easiest method of determining this is rolling them on a flat, smooth surface. Each pushrod should roll perfectly, without a bump or wobble. Even slightly askew pushrods cannot be used, meaning a new piece or a new set of pushrods must be procured.

Pushrods simply slide into place, typically through holes in the head, and rest upon the lifters. They are held in the correct position with the rocker arms. The majority of late-model engines use hydraulic flat-tappet or hydraulic roller-valve gear (easily identified by hydraulic-type lifters), meaning the installation is complete when preload is set between the pushrods and the rockers arms. Methods vary, depending on whether the engine uses adjustable rocker arms or non-adjustable arms (see the sidebar: "Setting Hydraulic-Cam Lifter Pre-Load" later in this chapter). Non-hydraulic, or solid-lifter, engines require a specified clearance relationship between the rocker arm and valvespring. This is called valve lash and must be performed accurately to ensure optimal and quiet performance. The factory service manual will provide the proper lash specifications and procedure.

Additional valvetrain-related inspections, such as piston-to-valve clearance and rocker arm clearance are necessary only if you have installed a camshaft with higher-than-stock lift specifications.

Crankshaft Damper/Pulley Installation

One of the most difficult aspects of the final engine assembly procedure is the installation of the crankshaft damper and/or pulley. For most engines, it is an extremely tight fit to install the damper/pulley on the crankshaft hub, often requiring an installation tool that can be rented from most auto parts stores. Some installations mandate that the crankshaft be held in place while the damper is torqued into position, typically requiring you to hold the crankshaft in place from the rear flange. There are other methods of installation, and you should consult the factory service manual for the manufacturer's recommendation.

Setup for Accurate Timing

Setting up the engine for accurate start-up ignition timing is very important during the final assembly steps. For most engines, this involves installing the distributor so that it is matched with top dead center on the number-1 cylinder. This should be done even on engines that must have the distributor removed for installation in the vehicle. Setting up timing is much easier with the engine on the stand rather than in the vehicle, so it's a procedure that should not be skipped in order to rush the final assembly.

Builders of engines with electronically controlled, distributorless ignition systems won't have to worry about setting the engine to top dead center; the camshaft and crankshaft are equipped with toothed wheels that are read by the complementing camshaft position and crankshaft position sensors.

They instantly determine the position of the components in relation to the pistons and set the timing automatically, assuming the crankshaft and camshaft(s) were lined up correctly during the assembly process. This greatly speeds the final assembly timeline, but foolproofs the ignition timing as well.

As mentioned throughout this book, attention to detail is essential for producing a well-built, accurately assembled engine. You should approach the final assembly with the same focus that was given the short block.

1 Install Cylinder Head Gaskets

It is a simple procedure, with no sealants or fasteners. The gasket is simply laid upon the deck; dowels in the deck hold the gasket in place for accurate location when the cylinder head is installed.

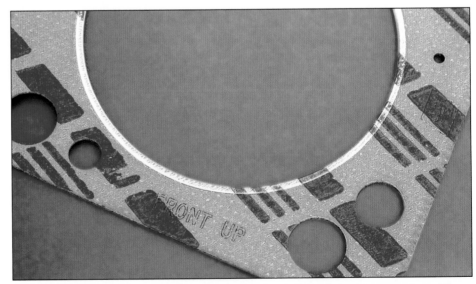

The only trick to head gasket installation is mounting it in the correct position. As this gasket shows, most are marked with indicators to make the task foolproof. A thicker gasket should be used if cylinder block deck and/or cylinder head machining has created a piston-to-valve clearance problem.

Important!

2 | Install Cylinder Heads

! With the head gasket in place, the head is carefully lowered into position. Typically, the heads are located with the same dowels that held on the cylinder head gasket. Dowels are very important on V-type engines because the heads are mounted on an angle, and the dowels will hold the heads in place while the builder installs the head fasteners. An alternative is positioning a V-engine so that the deck is on a level plane to install each head.

After the head was set upon the engine block of the Ford four-cylinder, the new camshaft was drenched in assembly lube as a precautionary measure. Minimizing friction at start-up is the key to long engine life.

Important!

4 | Install Cylinder Head Bolts

The head bolts can be coated lightly in motor oil prior to insertion. Dipping the threaded end of the bolts in a pan of oil is an easy method. Only a light coat of oil should be used—too much oil will pool at the bottom of the bolt hole and could cause problems during the final torque procedure, including a "hydraulic" issue that occurs because too much oil in the hole has nowhere to go. Typically, it damages the head bolt. Also, if the bolts protrude into a water jacket when installed, they should be coated with a sealer to prevent coolant leaks.

Professional Mechanic Tip **PRO TIP**

3 | Use New Head Bolts

All-new cylinder head bolts are recommended, even if the engine manufacturer suggests re-using the original bolts. This ensures a more accurate fastening and, therefore, positive cylinder head sealing.

*Torque Fasteners,
Professional Mechanic Tip*

5 | Torque Head Bolts to Factory Specification

The cylinder head bolts are tightened with a specific, factory-mandated sequence that should be referenced prior to the final fastening procedure. Generally, a center-out, clockwise pattern is used. In the case of this engine, a two-stage procedure (bolts were torqued in sequence in both primary and final stages) complemented the process. This process is essentially the same for all types of engines and care must be taken to perform the procedure correctly in order to ensure a correctly sealed engine.

6 | Install Pushrods (Cam-in-Block Engines Only)

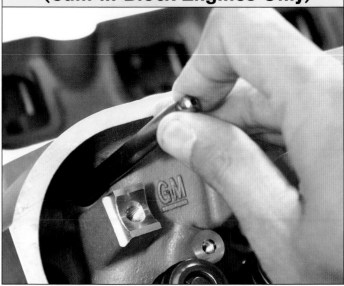

With the heads securely fastened, the pushrods are slipped into place. They slide through holes in the cylinder head and rest on the top of the lifters. Lubrication is not necessary. If the original pushrods are re-used, they should be inspected prior to installation by rolling them on a flat surface and checking for wobbles. Any pushrod that doesn't roll easily and flatly should be discarded.

7 | Install Rocker Arms (Cam-in-Block Engines Only)

After the pushrods, the rocker arms are next inserted. They install on brackets or cast-in towers on the cylinder head. The pushrod is positioned in the cupped section at the rear, and the tip is located on top of the valvespring. At this stage, they should be only lightly fastened. The tip and/or top of the spring should be lubricated. It may be necessary to rotate the engine with a breaker bar to provide enough clearance to install all of the rockers.

8 | Set Lifter Pre-Load (Cam-in-Block Engines Only)

Following the procedure outlined in the accompanying sidebar, "Setting Proper Hydraulic-Cam Lifter Pre-Load," the relationship between the rocker arms, pushrods, and lifters is adjusted. Engines with non-adjustable rocker arms require a different pre-load procedure (see Sidebar on page 89). Engines not equipped with a hydraulic cam and lifters will likely require valve lash adjustments at this stage. The builder should reference the factory service manual for the correct lash procedure and specifications.

Setting Proper Hydraulic Cam Lifter Preload

On cam-in-block engines with a hydraulic cam and lifters, it is necessary to set proper lifter preload to ensure engine performance at start-up and long-term valvetrain life. Incorrect or insufficient preload will result in excessive noise, rough or erratic idling, and, perhaps, insufficient engine vacuum.

Hydraulic Cam with Adjustable Rocker Arms

For hydraulic flat-tappet and hydraulic roller camshafts with adjustable rocker arms, preload is set by rotating the engine (starting with number-1 cylinder) until the exhaust valve/valvespring begins to move. At this point, the valve lash is set to zero, plus an additional half turn. Zero lash means there is no space or gap between the rocker arm and pushrod, so the preload is set by the pushrod touching the rocker arm plus the half-turn of the adjusting nut on the rocker arm. This procedure is repeated for each valve position.

Hydraulic Cam with Non-Adjustable Rocker Arms

For hydraulic flat-tappet and roller cams without adjustable rocker arms, the preload is set by rotating the engine until the intake and exhaust valves of a cylinder have opened and closed completely (with the rocker arms tightened to spec). After this has been completed, you must allow several minutes for the hydraulic lifters to bleed down. Then, using the cylinder head's outer rail as a guide, place a small reference mark on the pushrods.

Next, the rocker arms are loosened, but still able to support the pushrods. The pushrods should be free-standing on the lifters and have no preload (no pressure from the rocker arms). Now, the secondary marks are made on the pushrods using the same guide point from the cylinder head rail. The distance between the two marks on the pushrod indicates the preload and it should be between 0.020 inch and 0.040 inch. Because the rocker arms are non-adjustable, the preload should be the same for all of the engine's valves; therefore, only one intake valve and one exhaust valve should need to be checked.

Torque Fasteners

9 Torque Rocker Arms to Factory Specifications (Cam-in-Block Engines Only)

With the lifter pre-load set, the rocker arms are tightened to the specifications indicated by the manufacturer.

10 Install All Valve Cover Gaskets (All Engines)

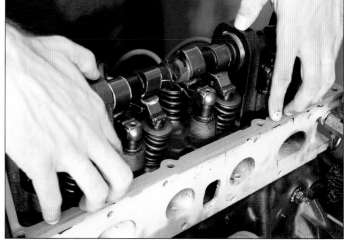

Valve cover gaskets are typically installed without liquid sealant, although a small amount can be used to hold the gasket in place. Some engines will locate the gasket on the valve cover itself prior to installation on the cylinder head. It is best to follow the recommendation of the service manual.

---

11 Install Valve Cover

Like the gasket, the valve cover is typically installed without sealant. The factory torque specifications of the fasteners should be precisely followed to prevent leaks. NOTE: It may be easier or preferred to install the valve covers on some V-type engines after the intake manifold is installed. This may be determined by the builder's experience during disassembly.

Overhead Cam Timing Chain/Belt Installation Tips

The timing belts or timing chains of overhead-cam V-design engines present unique installation challenges that aren't shared with the comparatively easy installation of belts or chains on cam-in-block engines. Procedures for achieving optimal chain or belt tension are often challenging. These procedures require adjustment of the tensioners and working with pulleys that connect the belt or chain between the cam gears on the cylinders heads. Also, specialized timing and/or tensioning tools are required on many engines that were OEM equipment during the last 20 years.

Here are some general guidelines to follow when preparing an overhead-cam engine for start-up:

• Do not re-use the original timing belt(s) or chain(s) because undetectable stretching can affect performance and ignition timing.

• Use only belts made of OE-quality HSN (highly saturated nitrile) material.

• Check the factory repair manual for installation/removal tools or tensioner tools and use them. Forc-ing the belt or chain without the recommended tool will likely result in frustration, failure, or both.

• Double-check the correct installation of cam gears/sprockets, thrust washers, etc. Backward, misaligned, or incorrectly installed parts can result in incorrect belt or chain installation and, consequently, incorrect timing.

• Do not attempt to stretch the belt in order to install it. Timing belts are not designed to stretch. If the belt doesn't slip over the sprockets, double-check the other components of the timing system.

• Check the repair manual for tension specs. Obviously, a loose belt or chain is problematic, and it may cause the belt to jump a tooth or two, affecting timing; a too-tight belt can wear prematurely and/or affect engine timing and operation.

• Check for special camshaft positioning tools to be used on dual-overhead-cam engines, which hold the camshafts in each head in correct relation to one another during belt/chain installation.

Important!

12 Install Timing Chain/Belt (Cam-in-Block Engines Only)

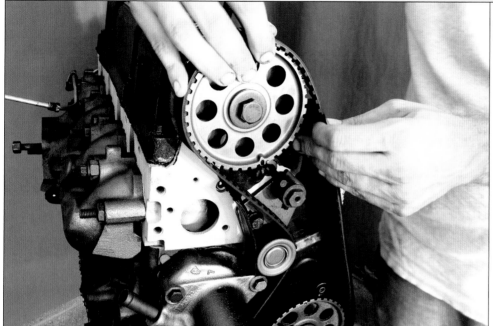

! *With the cylinder head(s) secure on an overhead-cam engine, the timing chain/belt can be attached. The factory service manual should be consulted to corroborate the correct position of line-up marks on the crank sprocket, cam sprocket, and, if equipped (as seen here), the auxiliary shaft sprocket. The chain or belt must be carefully slipped on with the cam and/or auxiliary shaft sprockets held in place to prevent them from rotating. If the marks are misaligned after the belt is installed, the belt should be removed and the process repeated.*

13 Install Crank-Driven Oil Pump or Water Pump (If Equipped)

Some late-model engines—particularly those with a distributorless ignition—use a crankshaft-driven oil pump or water pump, known as a gerotor-type pump. It is installed over the crankshaft hub after the timing chain is attached. An oil pump on a GM LS engine is shown here.

Torque Fasteners

14 Torque Oil Pump Bolts

The attachment of the GM gerotor oil pump illustrates the use of torque-to-yield fasteners, which requires a torque-angle meter to achieve the factory specification. Note the "18.0" reading on the torque wrench in the photo; it indicates the 18-degree specification for the oil pump fasteners. The digital Snap-on tool shown here is a professional item that allows both conventional ft-lb/Nm readings and torque angle readings.

Torque Fasteners

15 Install Front Cover (Cam-in-Block Engines Only)

With the timing chain and crank-driven oil pump installed, the engine's front cover is secured to the block in preparation for the crankshaft damper. Following the manufacturer's torque specification is important to prevent an oil leak.

17 Torque Crankshaft Damper Bolt

Torque Fasteners

After the damper is pressed onto the crankshaft hub, it is secured with one or more bolts. In the case of the GM engine shown here, it is held in place with one larger bolt that threads into the end of the crankshaft. Achieving the proper final torque specification requires immobilizing the crankshaft, usually by affixing some sort of brace to the rear flange of the crankshaft. Methods will vary, depending on the engine.

16 Install Crankshaft Damper

Special Tool

Installation of the pulley may require a pulley installer/remover for press-on parts. The damper/pulley (pictured) is pressed onto the crankshaft hub with a threaded rod that installs on the end of the crankshaft. Wrenching down the rod pushes the damper onto the crank hub.

18 Install Camshaft Position Sensor (Distributorless Engines Only)

With the front cover installed, the camshaft position sensor is attached to the cover. This sensor is used only on distributorless engines. This cam-in-block GM engine uses a single sensor; overhead-cam V-type engines will use at least one sensor for each camshaft.

Important!

19 Install Crankshaft Pulley

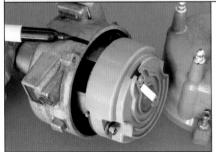

! The previous six photos showed installation procedures on a GM LS engine. Here, the crankshaft pulley is installed on the Ford 4-cylinder used primarily throughout the book. Its installation was a simple bolt-on affair. With the timing marks lined up on the sprockets and the timing belt installed, the crankshaft pulley is installed in preparation for locating top dead center (TDC) on the number-1 cylinder. When TDC is determined, a white paint mark will be made on the pulley to aid ignition timing.

20 Install Distributor to Locate Top Dead Center on Number-1 Cylinder

Insert the distributor as close as possible to the scribed marks made during the disassembly procedure. The distributor should be lightly fastened, but it remains hand adjustable. The goal is locating TDC on the number-1 cylinder, which is the forward-most cylinder on an inline engine and the forward-most cylinder on the right-hand side of a V-type engine.

21 Locate Top Dead Center on Number-1 Cylinder and Mark Distributor

Methods vary among engine types, but the procedure is largely the same: To find top dead center on the number-1 cylinder, the engine is rotated until the number-1 piston reaches its highest point, and the distributor rotor is pointed in the position that corresponds with the number-1 terminal on the distributor cap. When this is achieved, the distributor can be removed (if necessary) and the distributor case marked. If the distributor does not require removal to finish the engine assembly, it should be left in place. Also, the crankshaft-pulley timing mark should be painted to provide a reference point at start-up for setting the ignition timing.

22 Install Timing Belt Cover (Overhead Cam Engines

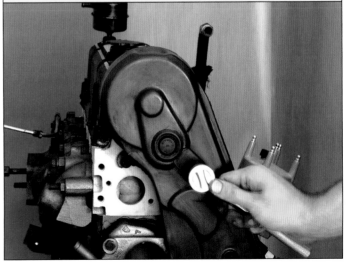

When you are sure the timing belt is installed correctly and top dead center on the number-1 cylinder is determined, the timing cover can be attached to the front of the engine.

23 | Install Exhaust Manifolds

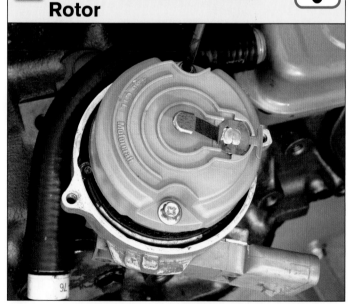

To prevent damaging the spark plugs, it may be easier on some engines to install the exhaust manifold(s) prior to installing the spark plugs and wires. New gaskets are used and typically don't require any sealant, but a couple small daubs of RTV can be used to hold the gasket in place.

24 | Prepare to Install Distributor, Spark Plugs and Wires

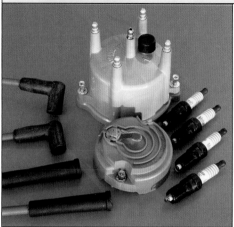

The distributor can be re-installed at this stage of the assembly process, if it was removed after locating TDC and doesn't require installation after the engine is in the vehicle. And while not necessary, a new distributor cap, rotor, spark plugs, and spark plug wires are a wise investment. NOTE: On some engines, particularly small-block and big-block Chevy engines, the intake manifold requires installation before the steps outlined here are attempted.

Important!

25 | Install New Distributor Rotor

On some engines, the rotor simply presses into place, while others (seen here) are screwed into place. Regardless, the builder must make sure the rotor matches the position indicated during the determination of top dead center.

26 | Install Distributor Cap

Most replacement caps are marked with the number-1 position, but it is also helpful for spark plug wire routing to mark the terminal position for every cylinder. Because the intake manifold and other components still require installation, the plug wires are not installed at this time.

27 Install Spark Plugs

The plugs can be threaded into place after the electrode gap is checked against the engine manufacturer's recommended specification. Anti-seize compound should be applied to the spark plug threads for plugs installed in aluminum heads. This helps prevent galling or cross-threading problems that can occur with the comparatively soft aluminum material.

28 Install Intake Manifold Assembly

Professional Mechanic Tip

The intake manifold assembly simply attaches to the engine with a new gasket between it and the cylinder head. Typical of most modern, port-injected engines, this assembly includes the fuel injectors, fuel rail, and fuel pressure regulator. Installing these components as an integrated assembly saves time.

The intake system on this engine is capped with the throttle body. Some engines' intake assemblies include the throttle body, making this step unnecessary. At this point in the assembly of a carbureted engine, the carburetor can be installed.

On V-type engines, the installation of the intake manifold may be affected by the cylinder head machining work, which can slightly alter the location of the manifold bolt holes in relation to the manifold. If the manifold bolts turn easily into the holes, there may be a misalignment issue. If that is the case, thicker intake manifold gaskets should solve the problem.

Like many late-model, fuel-injected inline-type engines, this engine's intake system consists of lower and upper sections. The upper section is installed after the lower section is fastened per factory specifications.

29 Install Spark Plug Wires

With the intake manifold and related hardware installed, the spark plug wires can be routed over or around the engine, as necessary.

On engines without a distributor, the ignition coils are typically mounted near the spark plugs. On this GM LS engine, for example, the coils mount to the valve cover and use very short plug wires between the coils and plugs. The coils are then connected to the ignition harness when the engine is installed in the vehicle.

30 Install Coolant Thermostat

On some engines (seen here) the thermostat installs on the water neck, while other engines have the thermostat installed directly on the intake manifold or a cylinder head. Sealant should not be used when installing the thermostat; it should simply press in place.

31 Install Water Neck

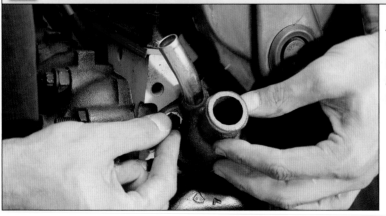

A gasket is typically required when installing the water neck, and a small amount of sealant can be used to hold the gasket in place. However, care must be taken to avoid sealant spreading out into the water passage and impeding the coolant flow.

Professional Mechanic Tip, Important! [PRO TIP] [!]

32 Install Water Neck

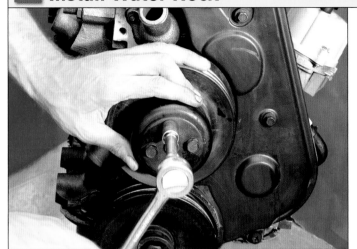

[PRO TIP] [!] *As the end of the assembly draws nearer, final assembly details include items such as drive pulleys. Thread locker should be used on the fasteners. You should be cognizant of the disassembly process because some accessories must be removed and reinstalled in a specific sequence to prevent interference with one another during assembly.*

Other installation items include the alternator bracket (seen here). Again, each engine's accessories vary and you should generally follow the reverse of the disassembly procedure. Also of note here, the alternator bracket, along with the other accessories and their brackets, has been cleaned prior to re-installation. You should not overlook cleaning these items in order to speed up the project.

Important! [!]

33 Install Turbocharger (If Required)

[!] *The engine depicted throughout this book is equipped with a turbocharger. It was re-installed after returning from a service that disassembled and rebuilt the compressor. The procedure is generally a*

straightforward, bolt-on step, but if the turbocharger has been rebuilt or is all new, the orientation of the two halves (the inlet side and the outlet side) should be checked so that they match the orientation of the turbocharger when it was removed. This is important because the connection of various fasteners, hoses, and tubes on the turbo depend on the "just-right" orientation. If the orientation is incorrect, the inlet or outlet side of the turbocharger unit can typically be loosened in order to "clock" the halves to the correct positions.

The turbocharger blows into the engine through an intake tube connected to the throttle body. This connection provides guidance as to whether the installed orientation of the turbo is correct. If the outlet of the turbo does not line up with the intake tube, the turbocharger's inlet/outlet orientation will require adjustment.

34 Prime and Install Oil Filter

The filter is filled with oil before installation to ensure the engine is primed with oil as quickly as possible after start-up.

After installing the oil filter, the engine can be filled with oil, or the job can wait until the engine is in the vehicle. If the builder waits, extreme care should be taken to ensure the engine is not started before the crankcase is filled.

Important!

35 Install Engine Mounting Brackets

Installing the engine mount brackets is the finishing touch on the engine assembly. With them in place, the engine assembly is finalized. With some engines, the brackets may install on the chassis, making this step unnecessary.

It should be noted that not every single item installed on the engine was shown in this chapter. Various hoses and cables, such as the starter cable, were installed without note because they were self-explanatory and very specific to this particular engine, but they are characteristic of the details required to finish every engine assembly. The assembled engine looks almost brand new and is ready for installation in the vehicle. That part of the project is covered in Chapter 7.

ENGINE INSTALLATION

Tools and Materials Required

- Shop crane
- Floor jack
- Oil dry
- Sockets, including deep-wells
- Wrenches
- Screwdrivers/nut drivers

The endgame in the project starts with the reinstallation of the engine. It is simple to say the installation process is the reverse of the removal procedure, but that is not entirely accurate. There are details specific to the installation and procedures not encountered during the removal stage. Throughout this chapter, the general procedures for the installation are outlined, but, as mentioned throughout the book, it is impossible to depict the specific sequence and details of all engines. At this stage in the project, however, there are no procedures that are specific to inline- or V-type engines; with overhead-cam or cam-in-block engines, the installation procedure is largely universal.

If you plan to install the engine with the transmission attached to the engine (as seen in this chapter), you will likely need assistance to guide the engine/transmission assembly over the front of the vehicle and into the engine compartment. And while it was recommended to lift the vehicle off the garage floor during the engine removal stage, most vehicles don't need to be raised to accept the rebuilt engine. However, you may find it more helpful to do so, particularly when bolting up the transmission.

As was the case during the engine's removal, take care to ensure adequate clearance over the nose of the vehicle as the engine is pushed into place, as well as make sure nothing impedes the engine as it is lowered into the chassis. This means checking that tied-off accessories, such as the power steering pump, throttle cable, etc., haven't shifted and fallen into the path of the engine. It is also wise to cover the nose of the vehicle with towels, a tarp, or something else that will serve as a barrier between the paint and the hard edges of the engine.

After a successful engine removal, the installation process for rear-wheel-drive engine/transmission combinations should seem relatively easy and straightforward. The key is proceeding in measured steps that simultaneously lower the engine and push the transmission under the vehicle (on rear-drive vehicles). At this time the assistance of another person is very important and helpful; one person should control the crane and the other should guide the engine and push the assembly down and under the transmission tunnel. It doesn't take much muscle to do this, but it is difficult to perform single-handedly. This "down and back" method continues until the engine has seated on the mounting points and the transmission is located correctly. Because of the severe downward angle of the transmission, its tailshaft would likely hit the shop floor before the engine is seated on the mounts. A floor jack pushed under the car—it may be helpful to raise the vehicle for this—can hold the transmission tailshaft and can be easily pushed to help guide the transmission into position as the engine is lowered.

The installation approach angle of the engine and transmission in a rear-drive vehicle may affect your decision to pre-fill a manual transmission with fluid. It is likely that some fluid will leak during the installation, but it may be ultimately easier to pre-fill the transmission for vehicles with inadequate access to the fill hole. Generally, automatic transmissions don't have this problem because they have a dipstick tube that can serve as a fill hole after the transmission has been installed.

The installation process for front-drive configurations and rear-drive vehicles with the transmission *not* attached to the engine is, generally speaking, a simple "straight down" method that can be performed by one person. In all cases, however, some adjustments may be required when the engine reaches the mounting points. The engine should be checked for level to ensure it is sitting squarely in or on the mounts. This should be done before the mounting bolts are tightened.

Component Hook-Up

When the engine is installed in the chassis and bolted in place, the task of reconnecting myriad lines, hoses, electrical connectors, and other components comes next. It is a painstaking, time-consuming part of the project that requires your full attention. Reference photos taken during the removal and disassembly stages will provide invaluable information and help ensure all the necessary connections and hook-ups have been made. Again, you should reference the factory service manual to determine the sequence of the installation steps or special tools required to facilitate the installation.

A quick reminder of the primary components and connections, in order of installation, includes:

Starter: Unless the starter was installed with the transmission during the engine's installation, it should be bolted up first because it is generally located low on the engine, and it may be more accessible if the vehicle is still on jack stands. Also, reconnected wires or hoses may make it more difficult to access the starter's location later. Don't forget to route the starter's primary lead to the starter relay or solenoid (if necessary).

Heater hoses: Reconnect the heater hoses between the firewall inlet/outlet ports and the engine. Inspect them for cracks or other wear and replace them as necessary.

Fuel line: Connect the fuel feed line to the carburetor or, on a fuel-injected engine, the fuel rail. The high-pressure systems of fuel-injected engines typically use push-on connectors or clips to secure the line. Check for excessive play or broken clips at the connection point and repair/replace as necessary.

Fuel filter: It's located on the engine or even in the engine compartment, but replacing the fuel filter is cheap insurance for a fresh engine.

Cooler lines: These circulate transmission and/or engine oil.

Return line: Many fuel-injected engines also have a fuel return line that goes bank to the fuel tank. Don't forget to connect it; it looks much like the fuel feed line, but is sometimes slightly smaller in diameter.

Throttle cable: Reconnect the throttle cable and/or linkage to the carburetor or throttle body. It should simply "pop" into position.

Wiring harnesses: It would be impossible to list all the possible wiring harnesses' connections found under the hoods of cars, but most are obvious and their corresponding plugs on the engine or chassis typically won't fit into any other harness. Reference photos are very helpful here because often the problem isn't matching a connector to its plug, but finding and completing all of the connections. Use your hands to follow wiring harnesses' leads to make sure they have a corresponding connector plugged in. However, some vehicles have harness connections with no corresponding plug-ins. This could be due to options that weren't included on the vehicle, such as air conditioning, or the harness could be a port for the engine's computers or diagnostic equipment. Again, rely on your reference photos and shop manual to make sure all of the necessary electrical connections are completed.

Vacuum lines and emissions equipment: Like electrical connections, most engines have a variety of vacuum hoses and emissions equipment. Check your shop manual to ensure all of the necessary hoses are pushed or clamped in place. They should also be inspected for cracks or holes that could cause a vacuum leak—this is a problem that can manifest itself even if the engine didn't have a prior history of vacuum leaks. The act of disconnection and reconnection can be hard on older vacuum lines, causing stiff or brittle lines to crack.

Accessories: When the wiring and vacuum lines are connected, move to the front of the engine and begin re-installing the engine-driven accessories, such as the alternator, power steering pump, and, on some vehicles, the AIR (smog) pump. Don't forget to re-connect the wiring at the rear of the alternator, and, if the power steering pump was left in the chassis during the engine rebuilding process, check the hoses for leaks and carefully install it so as not to damage the hose ends.

Air conditioner: If the air-conditioning system was discharged during the engine removal process, re-install the pump and re-connect the necessary lines. The system can be re-charged after the engine is broken-in and the vehicle is in running order. If the pump was removed without discharging the system, carefully install it, but check the lines for leaks.

Pulleys and/or drive belts: With the accessories in place, re-install the V-belts or serpentine belt. Replacing the old belt(s) with a new one is a good idea. The tensioner pulley (if equipped) should be inspected, too, to ensure it is not worn.

Air intake system: On port fuel-injected engines, connect the air intake tube between the throttle body and air cleaner. Wait to install the air cleaner on a carbureted or TBI-style injected engine until start-up—it will leave more open space to work with under the hood.

Mass air sensor: Don't forget to connect the wiring harness at the sensor on a mass-air-equipped engine.

MAP sensor line: This is often a vacuum line connected to a port on or near the firewall. It is a very important connection, as it will prevent the engine from running properly if left unconnected.

Ground lines: Many otherwise perfect start-ups are thwarted by a neglected chassis ground cable. Don't forget the battery ground cable,

either, as it is often disconnected during the engine removal stage.

Exhaust system: Reconnect the exhaust system prior to start-up. On some systems, this may require a new "donut": the circular gasket that is located between the exhaust manifold and exhaust down pipe. In fact, if the exhaust system hasn't been replaced for a long time, a new donut is probably a wise investment toward ensuring a leak-free exhaust system.

While every effort has been made to depict the most universal aspects of the installation configuration and emissions system, the control system is different for almost every engine. Therefore, I cannot demonstrate the number of connections and the sequence for all engines. As time has progressed, the number of hoses, vacuum lines, and connectors under the hood has decreased, meaning some builders will encounter a relatively easy hook-up process, while others will be saddled with a veritable "plumber's nightmare" of emissions-related hoses and lines.

Finally, it is a good idea to inspect the electrical connections and wires for immediate damage or a general worn-out appearance, especially if you are working on an older vehicle. Wiring covers can become brittle over time, leading to exposed wires that can cause shorts. In fact, these conditions can appear even though, prior to the engine project, there were no problems. The movement and handling of the wires during the project can cause brittle wires or connections to break.

Transmission Connections and Clutch Adjustment

After the engine and its requisite hoses, other lines, and electrical

components have been connected, the transmission must be connected, too. For automatic transmissions, this involves the reconnection of the speedometer and/or vehicle speed sensor, the automatic shifter linkage, fluid lines (if equipped with a transmission cooler), and, for electronically controlled transmissions, the powertrain control module. The same goes for a manual transmission, but it also requires the reconnection of the clutch pedal linkage and a clutch adjustment (for transmissions with a hydraulic clutch, but no self-adjusting system).

Although clutch systems and adjustment procedures vary from vehicle to vehicle, there are basic steps to follow in order to ensure the clutch engages smoothly and accurately; this includes ensuring adequate take-up free play in the pedal. The vehicle's service manual should outline the procedure and provide the recommended free play specification. In most cases, the clutch system has one or more adjustable fixtures located on the firewall, either on the engine side or under the dashboard. The clutch can be adjusted to the factory specs by loosening these fixtures and following the service manual's guidelines.

An incorrectly adjusted clutch will manifest itself in a number of ways, including difficulty engaging gears, engaging higher after the engine is warmed up, clunking during gear changes, or a lack of resistance when the clutch pedal is pushed more than 1 inch. These problems are generally caused by inadequate free play that doesn't allow the hydraulic fluid to return to the clutch master cylinder. In turn, the fluid heats up and expands through the lines, causing the clutch to release and adversely affect performance.

The transmission must also be reconnected to the drive wheels. This means reinstalling the driveshaft on a rear-drive car and connecting the transmission to the axle on a front-driver. Finally, if the transmission wasn't filled prior to installation, it should be topped off with the appropriate manufacturer-recommended fluid.

Safety Step

1 Attach Shop Crane to Engine

With the engine still on the stand, the shop crane re-enters the project. The lifting chains are attached to the engine in preparation for removing the engine from the stand. Seen here, a load leveler is used to provide better balance of the engine/transmission assembly during installation.

Torque Fasteners

3 Install Flywheel or Flexplate

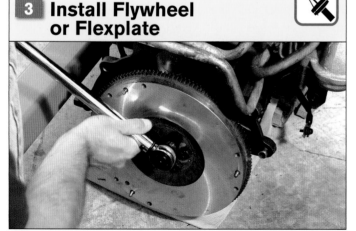

The engine will likely need to be lowered to the ground or braced somehow in order to fasten the flywheel/flexplate bolts to the factory torque specification. Loctite Red thread locker is recommended for the flywheel/flexplate bolts.

2 Remove Engine from Engine Stand

The engine stand mounting-bracket is unbolted from the rear of the engine, releasing the engine from the stand.

4 Clean Flywheel Surface

To ensure a clean, oil-free material for the clutch plate, the flywheel surface is wiped with a lint-free rag that has been sprayed with brake cleaner.

5 Prepare to Install New Clutch (Manual Transmission Only)

A new clutch kit is recommended for manual-transmission vehicles. The kit typically includes a clutch disc, pressure plate, clutch release bearing, pilot bushing, and bearing and installation/alignment (pilot) tool.

Torque Fasteners, Professional Mechanic Tip

7 Install New Clutch and Pressure Plate (Manual Transmission Only)

The clutch disc fits inside the pressure plate and the pair is mated to the flywheel. The plastic installation tool included with the kit correctly aligns and holds the assembly in place while the pressure plate is bolted to the flywheel. It simply pulls free when the clutch/ pressure plate assembly is installed. There is a torque spec for the bolts that must be followed. In this photo, the builder's right hand is on the alignment tool, as he is ready to pull it out after securing the assembly to the flywheel.

6 Clean New Pressure Plate (Manual Transmission Only)

Prior to installation, the new pressure plate is cleaned in the same manner as the flywheel. A new pressure plate ensures adequate leverage is used on the new clutch.

8 Install Bellhousing (Manual Transmission Only)

The bellhousing slips over the clutch assembly and should include the new pilot bearing/release bearing that came with the clutch kit.

9 Install Transmission

If the transmission is to be installed as an assembly with the engine, it is time to join them. As with the disassembly procedure, a floor jack is used to maneuver the transmission to the bellhousing. A manual transmission is shown here, but an automatic transmission installation would also include the installation of the torque converter (see the next two photos for converter installation tips).

Precision Measurement

11 Install Torque Converter (Automatic Transmission Only)

The converter is then slipped on to the transmission's input shaft. Seating the converter correctly can be a trial-and-error process and the manufacturer has installation specifications regarding the run out measurement of the drive plate and the converter hub sleeve. A spot-on converter installation is necessary to prevent vibration and fluid leaks.

Important!

10 Fill Torque Converter with Fluid (Automatic Transmission Only)

If the automatic transmission was serviced as part of the rebuild project, it will likely have received a new torque converter or a flushed original converter. (The converters of lock-up-style transmissions cannot be serviced and must be replaced.) To prepare the transmission for installation, automatic transmission fluid is poured into the new or flushed converter.

12 Plug Transmission to Tailshaft

Insert a plug into the transmission tailshaft to prevent fluid leakage. If the transmission is to be pre-filled with fluid prior to installation, other holes in the transmission should be plugged or taped over to prevent leaking, too. Even with these precautions, fluid is likely to leak out somewhere. Prepare the shop floor under the vehicle with oil dry or a flat piece of cardboard to catch the fluid.

13 Fill Transmission with Fluid

Following the manufacturer's fluid recommendation, the transmission is filled prior to installation. The gamble here is that is much easier to fill the transmission while it is still out of the vehicle, but the builder risks significant leakage if the engine/transmission assembly is inserted at a severe angle or if any of the plugs fail or fall out.

14 Prepare Vehicle for Engine Installation

Before the engine is pushed into the installation position, the vehicle is readied by raising the hood as far as possible and clearing tools, parts, and other items from the path of the shop crane.

The engine compartment is also inspected prior to the engine's installation to ensure the ancillary components, such as the power steering pump, hoses, and hard lines are out of the way. As with various engine parts and accessories, the engine compartment should be cleaned prior to receiving the rebuilt engine. This makes the installation easier and a lot less messy.

15 Raise Engine and Push It into Position

With the vehicle ready to accept the engine, it can be jacked up with the crane and slowly, carefully pushed into position. The weight of the transmission will pull the assembly downward at the rear, requiring it to be raised quite high to clear the grille/radiator core support area of the vehicle.

---

16 Protect Car Body

Important!

! *Note the towels placed on the vehicle in this photo. This helps prevent scratching should the assembly inadvertently come into contact with the car body, as well as prevent any fluid from dripping onto the body.*

18 Continue Lowering Engine into Vehicle

As the engine continues to be lowered, it is pushed farther back into the engine compartment, and the transmission tailshaft moves back into the transmission tunnel. You should continue with the down and back method, inching down the engine while simultaneously pushing the assembly back, until the engine is centered over the engine mounting points.

17 Begin Lowering Engine into Vehicle

The installation procedure for longitudinally located engines (mostly rear-drive vehicles) uses the "down and back" method, lowering the engine slowly after it is pushed as far back in the engine compartment as possible. It should be lowered inch by inch, but as this photo illustrates, it is clear the engine is not centered over the engine mounts. On vehicles with a transverse-mounted engine (mostly front-drive vehicles), the builder must take care to line up the engine over the center of the engine compartment, making minor fore/aft and sideways adjustments as the engine lowers further into the chassis.

Professional Mechanic Tip

19 Guide Transmission with Floor Jack (Longitudinal Arrangements)

PRO TIP

PRO TIP *When the engine/transmission assembly is lowered significantly into the vehicle, the transmission must be guided into position before it reaches the ground. A floor jack is the perfect tool for this because the transmission tailshaft rests on the jack pad as it is lowered. The jack is maneuvered along with the engine, guiding the transmission into the correct, horizontal position, along with the engine.*

20 Guide Engine onto Mounting Points

With the engine lowered almost completely into the engine compartment, attention must be paid to guide the engine mounts to the mounting points on the chassis. At this point, the engine should be low enough in the engine compartment and free of interfering components that would prevent the engine from being easily lowered into the position. The transmission should be close to its final position.

Professional Mechanic Tip **PRO TIP**

21 Guide Transmission with a Floor Jack (Longitudinal Arrangements)

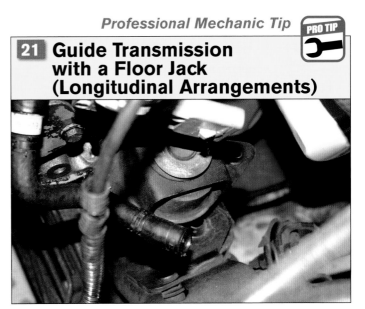

PRO TIP In this photo, the engine mount is only slightly askew from the mounting point (seen as the raised, cone-shaped stamping located at the center of the photo). At this point, the engine is lowered to the point of barely touching the mounting points and the builder muscles the engine onto the points. The unmistakable sound and feeling of a male/female component match indicates the engine is located on the mounting points.

Important! **!**

22 Check Engine's Level

! Although the engine may be seated on its mounting points, it may not be seated correctly. A quick check with a level at the front of the engine shows whether this is the case. As the level in this photo indicates, the engine needs a slight adjustment; usually, this involves only a push to the right or left to center the engine perfectly on the mounting points. NOTE: The level should be checked on the engine's transverse (side to side) plane because almost all engines are mounted on a slight front-to-rear angle.

23 Install Engine Mount Fasteners

When the engine is on the mounting points, it is simply attached with the bolts that thread through the chassis points and engine-mounted brackets.

24 Remove Shop Crane

Once the engine is securely mounted and the lifting chains are removed, the shop crane is pulled away from the vehicle. If you nailed the engine assembly process correctly, it should be the last time the crane is seen during the project.

Critical Inspection

26 Visually Inspect Engine

Prior to reconnecting the numerous hoses, lines, and electrical harnesses to the engine, visually inspect the engine to ensure nothing impedes the next steps, such as leaks, damaged engine compartment components, and the like. At this point, it is easier to remove the engine, if necessary, than disconnect the items later in the process.

25 Attach Transmission Crossmember

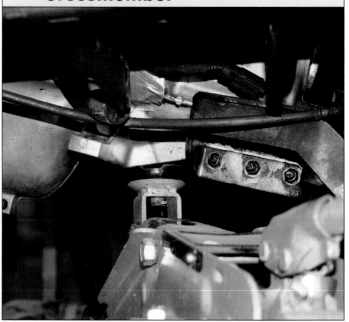

With the floor jack still holding the transmission in place, it is used to jack the transmission into the correct position so that the crossmember can be attached. This holds the transmission in the correct position, allowing the clutch cable and shifter to be re-installed.

27 Consult Reference Photos

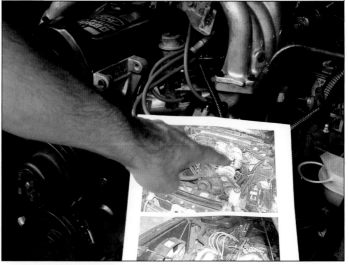

The mounting position of hoses, lines, and connections that seemed so very self-explanatory during the engine removal stage may now be impossible to discern. The routing and sequence of the connections is made infinitely easier if you consult reference photos taken during the removal stage.

28 Connect Fuel Supply

The fuel line is pushed onto the fuel rail or carburetor. On typical fuel injection systems, the high-pressure fuel line locks into place with a positive click. A slight tug on the line confirms it is firmly in place. Carbureted engines use fuel lines that are typically secured with a nut-type fastener that bolts up to the fuel inlet of the carburetor.

29 Connect Throttle Assembly

Fuel-injected and carbureted applications use throttle systems that are attached largely the same. Engines with electronically controlled throttles do not have a cable-operated throttle system and, thus, will not have a similar system to affix to the throttle body.

30 Connect Ignition System

On most contemporary, computer-controlled vehicles, this involves plugging in a harness from the chassis-based ignition controller and the electronically controlled distributor. Of course, the coil wire must be connected between the coil and distributor. On distributorless systems, the ignition coils are simply connected to the controller; on older, non-electronic systems, the distributor may be connected to the chassis or engine via a vacuum hose.

Professional Mechanic Tip PRO TIP

31 Install Alternator, Power Steering Pump and Other Engine-Driven Accessories

At the front of the engine, the driven accessories are bolted in place. If care was taken, the power steering pump can be re-positioned without leaking. The disassembly reference photos should be consulted to check for the correct orientation of the components and/or their mounting brackets. Also check that the pulleys line up on the same plane after installation in order to ensure trouble-free routing of the drive belt(s). A misaligned pulley will cause a belt routing problem that will be harder to fix after more of the underhood components are installed.

32 Install Air Conditioning Assembly

Important! **!**

! *Along with the alternator, power steering pump, and other accessories, the air conditioning system (if equipped) is next. The system should not have been discharged during the removal process. As always, care must be taken to avoid cracking or breaking the lines. If these precautions were followed, it should still provide cold-air comfort when the engine is started.*

33 Install Drive Belts

With the front-end accessories in place, the V-belt(s) or serpentine belt is installed. Adjust the alternator or belt tensioner to allow enough slack to route the belt around all of the pulleys. Check the tension after the installation and adjust it, as necessary.

Professional Mechanic Tip

34 Install Starter **PRO TIP**

PRO TIP *You typically install the starter from the bottom of the engine compartment because it is mounted at the lower corner of the engine and meshes with the flywheel or flexplate. It is a good idea to test the starter prior to installation to ensure it is in working condition. After it is installed, the starter should be connected to the starter cable. Testing the starter can be accomplished at most auto parts stores for free.*

35 Install Air Intake or Air Cleaner

On fuel-injected vehicles, this step involves reconnecting the air intake tube between the engine and chassis-mounted air cleaner assembly. On carbureted and TBI-style engines, it involves reinstalling the air cleaner system on the engine.

36 Connect Electrical Connections and Install Hoses

Important!

Because every engine is different, it is impossible to name and show the location of the various electrical connectors, emissions hoses, and other lines that require installation. You should reference photos in the factory service manual to ensure all the appropriate connections have been made. If photos were taken during disassembly, the builder should also refer to these photos.

37 Install Heater Hoses

If the hoses are cracked, brittle, cut, or damaged, they need to be replaced. If they are in acceptable condition, the heater hoses can be reinstalled without replacement. They should simply slip back onto the inlet/outlet tubes protruding from the firewall and onto the corresponding inlet/outlet ports on the engine. A little lubricant swabbed on the inside of the tubes helps them slip on easily.

38 Connect Exhaust System

The exhaust system is pulled up to the exhaust manifold(s) and re-connected. Care must be taken with exhaust bolts, as they tend to become brittle over time. The builder shouldn't be surprised if on or more bolts or studs breaks, requiring new fasteners.

39 Connect All Exhaust System Sensors

If the exhaust oxygen sensor is located in the exhaust manifold or it was disconnected from the vehicle during the removal stage, it (or they) should be reconnected to the emissions control system at this point. This involves screwing the sensor into the exhaust tract, wrenching it tight, and connecting the sensor lead to the wiring harness.

40 Install Radiator

When little-to-no more work is required at the front of the engine, the radiator can be slipped into place. Don't fasten the radiator completely until the radiator hoses are installed. If overheating was a problem that prompted the engine rebuild in the first place, it's a good idea to upgrade the radiator to a higher-capacity unit. In the case of this car, the original two-core radiator was replaced with a three-core unit. The rebuilt engine's new water pump may also help prevent overheating.

41 Install Radiator Hoses, Overflow Tank Line and Connectors

With the radiator loosely installed, the radiator hoses are installed next. When the hoses are seated properly on the engine and radiator, the radiator hold-down brackets can be securely fastened, and the hose clamps securely tightened. Along with the radiator hoses is the hose that connects the radiator to the coolant overflow tank.

42 Install Cooling Fan

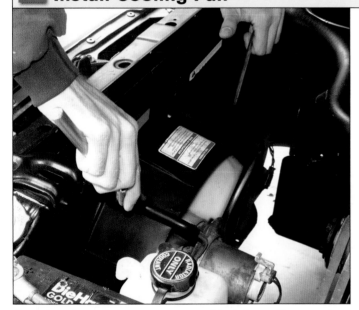

The electric cooling fan mounts behind the radiator and typically bolts to flanges on the radiator. If the engine uses an engine-driven fan, it should be installed before the radiator. This prevents the fan blades from inadvertently cutting into the radiator when it is lowered into place.

A simple yet very important connection to not overlook is the cooling fan controller. You should double-check to make sure it is plugged into the fan after installation.

43 Connect Chassis Ground Strap

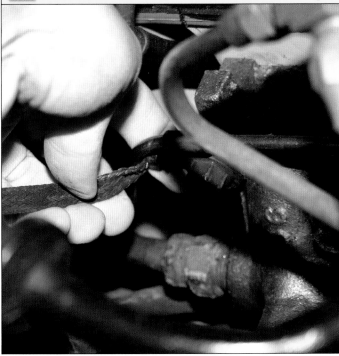

Another very easy component to overlook during the installation process is the chassis ground strap. It should be cleaned and attached to the engine block or an exhaust manifold; otherwise, the engine simply won't start. It won't even turn over.

45 Install Shifter (Manual Transmission Only)

Moving to the vehicle's interior, the shifter is reattached to the transmission, completing the installation of the transmission.

44 Connect Clutch Cable (Manual Transmission Only), Speedometer Cable and/or Other Transmission Connectors

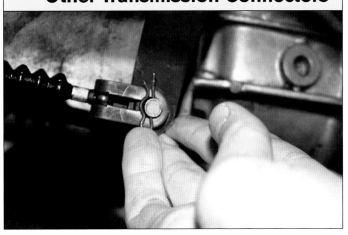

With the engine connections completed, the transmission and the clutch cable are reconnected to the transmission. The speedometer cable is pushed into the transmission and other electronic harnesses are connected, as necessary.

46 Install Driveshaft (Rear-Wheel-Drive Vehicles Only)

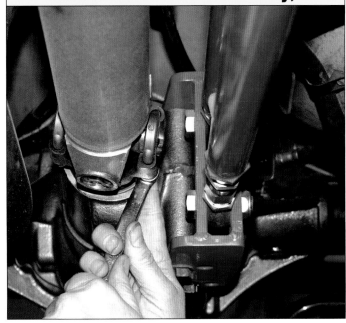

The final step in the engine/transmission assembly phase is the re-installation of the driveshaft on rear-drive vehicles. It simply slips back into the transmission and bolts up to the rear axle via the U-joint. Thread sealant is recommended for the U-joint bolts.

START-UP, TUNING AND BREAK-IN

Tools and Materials Required

- Oil and coolant
- Oil system priming tool
- Timing light

With the rebuilt engine installed and all of the various hoses, electrical connections, and other accessories re-connected, it is time to prepare the engine for starting, tuning, and the break-in procedures. This includes topping off the fluids (including the oil),

filling the radiator with coolant, priming the oil system, and, after the engine is started, setting the ignition timing.

Oil system priming is the most important task to perform before the engine is started. I suggest holding off on filling the cooling system until after the engine's oiling system has been primed and/or rolled over without spark or fuel (see next section). The roll-over period will be brief and not create appreciable heat in the engine, but if a dire condition

is detected—such as an engine that won't turn over or a severe oil leak—the engine can be worked on or removed much more easily without having to drain the cooling system.

After the engine is fired up for the first time, turn your attention to ensuring the ignition timing is set correctly and inspecting the engine compartment and floor beneath the engine for any signs of leaks. From there, the engine's break-in period starts, beginning with a test drive.

1 Top Off Fluids

Preparation for starting the engine starts with topping off the fluids, including filling the crankcase with oil.

2 Fill Radiator

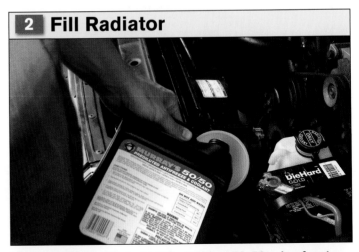

The radiator needs to be filled with a 50-50 mix of water and coolant, but it should wait until the oiling system has been primed, so that any problems that arise from the priming procedure won't require draining the new coolant.

3 Oil Priming

The oil priming tool simply slips into the chuck of an electric drill. The aluminum ring rests on the distributor hole in the cylinder block or intake manifold, steadying the tool during use. This type of tool can only be used on engines that have a distributor-driven oil pump.

To prime the oiling system with the priming tool, the distributor is removed and the tool is inserted. It locks onto the oil pump driveshaft and, when the drill is activated, the pump spins and distributes oil through the oiling circuit.

Oil System Priming

As the most important task performed prior to starting the engine, oil system priming is crucial to ensuring oil pressure is achieved and the reciprocating components are sufficiently lubricated at start-up. This means circulating oil throughout the engine and lubing the bearings, reciprocating parts, and other components. A variety of methods can be used, including using a priming tool or rolling over the engine without spark and/or fuel. Some methods are easier than others, and they are outlined in the next few paragraphs. But the bottom line is, the engine should *never* be started without an adequately primed oiling system. The factory service manual should provide guidance on the manufacturer's preferred method of priming.

Electric drill and priming tool

On many cam-in-block engines, particularly Ford V-8, Chevy V-8 and 90-degree V-6, and Pontiac V-8, the easiest and preferred method of priming involves removing the distributor and inserting a tool mounted to an electric drill that spins the oil pump, thereby pressuring the oil system. The priming tools are available from most auto parts stores and online parts retailers. Care must be taken to ensure the distributor is re-installed in the precise, pre-prime location, or the ignition timing could be significantly affected at start-up. If a pressure gauge is part of the vehicle's gauge package, the battery should be engaged and the priming should continue until the gauge shows normal oil pressure. If a pressure gauge isn't in the vehicle, the priming procedure should last at least 30 seconds to 1 minute.

Non-fire rollover method

Overhead-cam engines and engines with a distributorless ignition system cannot benefit from the electric drill priming method. These engines can generally be primed with one of two methods: vacuum priming, or non-fire roll-over. The non-fire roll-over method is the easiest and, in some cases, is likely the only option. It involves engaging the battery and "starting" the engine with either the fuel system or ignition coil disabled. Use the ignition key or a handheld starter switch to "start" the engine, causing the engine to roll over, but not actually start. The roll-over is only required

Professional Mechanic Tip **PRO TIP**

4 Roll-Over Priming Method

PRO TIP *Without a priming tool, the roll-over priming method begins with disabling either the ignition system or the fuel system. Here, the coil wire is disconnected, allowing the engine to be turned over without starting.*

5 Turn Key to "Start"

With the ignition or fuel system disabled, the ignition key is turned to the START position, allowing the starter to turn over the engine.

6 Check Oil Pressure Gauge

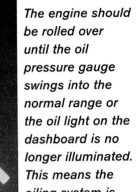

The engine should be rolled over until the oil pressure gauge swings into the normal range or the oil light on the dashboard is no longer illuminated. This means the oiling system is primed well enough to safely start the engine.

for a few seconds (roughly 15-second intervals), but it should be long enough to note whether the starter engaged without a problem and that the engine turned over easily. Rolling over the engine also ensures the starter is connected correctly, the oil system is primed, and that no other problems are immediately apparent.

Vacuum priming method

The other, more involved oil priming method for overhead-cam and distributorless engines involves forcing oil circulation through the engine with a vacuum pump. Power-operated pumps are available, but can be prove costly for the enthusiast who may only use it once. A vastly cheaper alternative involves using a garden-type pumping bottle—such as those used for spraying liquid fertilizer or weed killer—and an adapter to fit either the oil pump or oil filter housing. With the bottle filled with oil, you pump the oil into the engine. This pushes the oil through the entire oiling circuit, ensuring the bearings and reciprocating assembly is lubed. Once completed, the vacuum method can be augmented with the non-fire roll-over method to ensure normal oil pressure.

If no troublesome sounds, leaks, or odors were detected during the roll-over period, it's time to fill the cooling system and start the engine with the ignition enabled. NOTE: When the

7 Re-Connect Ignition or Fuel System and Start Engine

With the oil system primed, the radiator filled, and the ignition system hooked up, the engine can be turned over and started for the first time. If the ignition timing is close to accurate, the engine should fire more or less immediately.

8 Check Gauges

The dashboard gauges should be monitored closely for the first few minutes of the engine's operation, with coolant temperature and oil pressure being the most important items to watch.

engine is started, you will have to top off the system as the thermostat opens and the engine begins to ingest coolant.

Engine Start-Up

Some vehicles may have a specific start-up procedure, and you should check the service manual before turning the key. This could include a sustained idle period in which the engine cannot be turned off, or a regiment of RPM adjustments to break in a flat-tappet camshaft. But generally speaking, with a primed oiling system, a filled cooling system, and all the other necessary hoses and electrical connections hooked up, it is time to start the engine.

When the engine is started for the first time, you should look immediately at the dashboard gauges, checking that either the oil pressure gauge registers in the "normal" range or that the oil symbol light turns off quickly. If the gauge reads low or the oil light does not go out, the engine should be turned off *immediately*. Also, you should listen closely to the engine; if there is any indication of an unfamiliar sound, rattle, or metal-on-metal scraping noise, the engine should be turned off immediately.

If the engine sounds fine and the oil pressure proves adequate, the engine should be allowed to continue idling while you inspect the engine for leaks, loose parts or fasteners, or excessive vibration that could indicate a broken or incorrectly installed engine mount.

As the engine warms up, the thermostat will open and draw coolant into the engine; add coolant as necessary while the engine is idling. You should also check that the electric cooling fan kicks on when the engine warms up. It also helps to turn on the heater so that the new coolant will circulate through the entire system. This helps push trapped air out of the system, too.

Obviously, you should keep an eye on the coolant temperature gauge. First of all, it should be checked for functionality; if, after a few minutes, the gauge needle doesn't begin to move, you should check the lead wire on the temperature sensor to ensure it has been correctly installed. Also, after the engine begins to heat up, the gauge should be checked to verify the engine isn't getting too hot too quickly—a sign that there is either not enough coolant in the system or there is another problem, such as a faulty water pump.

Incorrectly installed water pump gaskets or insufficient water pump sealing are common causes of leaking on a rebuilt engine. As the engine continues to warm up, the water pump and the shop floor beneath it should be checked for signs of leaking coolant. Often, a problem in this area will become apparent very quickly. If a leak occurs, the engine should be turned off immediately, and the problem rectified before continuing with the break-in procedure.

For most applications, allow the re-built engine to run for 10 to 20 minutes before turning it off for the first time. This allows the pistons to begin seating in the bores and allows the cooling system to push water through the entire system. During this idling period, you should check and adjust the ignition timing.

When the engine is turned off the first time, check the oil level and inspect the underside of the car for leaks. If everything checks out, it's time for the road test break-in period.

Adjusting Valve Lash after Start-Up

Engines with a solid-lifter valvetrain may require valve lash adjustment after the engine is started for

Important!

9 Monitor Cooling System

Keep a close eye on the coolant temperature because the cooling system often requires additional coolant when the thermostat opens. If the odor of coolant or a leak appears, the engine needs to be turned off immediately. Also, if the coolant doesn't pull through the radiator relatively quickly and the temperature gauge reads too hot, the engine must be turned off immediately to check for a faulty water pump or thermostat.

the first time, and require periodic adjustments thereafter. If the lash was set during the engine assembly, it should be checked after the engine has run for a few hundred miles, or sooner if a loud ticking sound is audible. This step is not required for engines that use hydraulic lifters.

To adjust the valve lash in the vehicle, the battery should be disconnected. Remove the valve cover(s) to provide access to the rocker arms. The service manual should be consulted for the proper lash specifications, as well as any specific adjustment steps. (Lash inspection/adjustment is specified on some engines with a cylinder's lash checked only while another's valves are in overlap.)

The general adjustment procedure involves the following:

- Starting with cylinder number-1, rotate the engine until the piston is at top dead center (TDC). At this point, the rocker arms should exhibit a small amount of "play." If they don't, the valves may be overly tight or TDC is not achieved.
- A feeler gauge is inserted in the gap between the rocker arm and the top of the valvespring. If there is no gap, the valves are overly tight or TDC is not achieved.
- Following the service manual's specifications, a feeler gauge of the appropriate gap is inserted between the rocker arm and valvespring. Then, the lash is adjusted until the feeler gauge "drags" between the two components. In other words, the gauge is in contact with both the rocker arm and valvespring, but it can be pulled out. If the gauge is stuck between the components and cannot be pulled out, the lash is too tight.

- Repeat the process for all cylinders, making sure TDC is achieved at each cylinder.
- Reinstall the valve cover(s) and reconnect the battery.

Ignition Timing Adjustment

Assuming the distributor was installed correctly and the engine fired quickly and smoothly, setting timing involves relatively minor adjustments. Engines with distributorless ignition systems do not have manual timing adjustments; the engine controller sets their timing at start-up. It is very easy to determine incorrect timing when the engine is started. A slow start-up that requires extended cranking and/or a rattling/pinging sound when the engine is revved are immediate indicators that the timing is off. Also, hesitant starting, stumbling, backfiring, and the smell of unburned fuel can indicate severely misplaced timing. In that case, the distributor may be incorrectly installed.

Some builders intentionally set the distributor in an advanced position for the initial start to ensure a quick ignition but, regardless of the distributor's position, you need a timing light to adjust and set the timing. The service manual should provide the specifications for initial timing advance (the number of degrees before top dead center the spark plug should fire at idle), such as 10-degrees initial advance. Initial advance corresponds with an idle speed, so checking the tachometer is essential. If the vehicle's instrument panel doesn't have a tachometer, an aftermarket tach can be plugged in temporarily under the hood.

Here are the basic steps in using a timing light to check and adjust timing:

1. Connect the timing light. Typically, the timing light will have leads that connect to the battery posts and a connector that is clipped to the spark plug wire for cylinder number-1.

2. Point the timing light at the timing tab near the crankshaft pulley

10 Distributorless Engine Timing

Later-model engines with distributorless ignition systems, such as this GM LS V-8, do not require manual ignition timing inspection or adjustment. It is automatically set by the controller when the engine is started.

and pull the light's trigger to engage the strobe light. With the engine idling at the speed to correspond with initial timing, the timing light is pointed down toward the crankshaft pulley and the engine's fixed timing tab. Be cognizant of the timing light's leads, being careful to avoid entangling them in hoses or the cooling fan.

3. Check the relationship of the pulley's timing mark against the fixed timing tab. The timing light's strobe will "freeze" the timing mark on the pulley. It if is aligned straight up with the timing tab pointer, the ignition timing is correct and no further adjustments are required. If the timing marks *do not* line up, a timing adjustment is required.

4. To adjust the timing, the distributor is loosened enough so that it can be turned by hand. With slight movements, the distributor is turned until the timing marks line up when checked with the timing light. Typically, only slight adjustments are required to bring initial timing into specification. When the marks come into alignment, the distributor can be tightened; the timing is set.

When the ignition timing is correctly set, the engine should idle smoothly and rev without stumbling or pinging. When this is achieved, the engine is tuned sufficiently for the road test.

11 Timing Check for Distributor-Equipped Engines

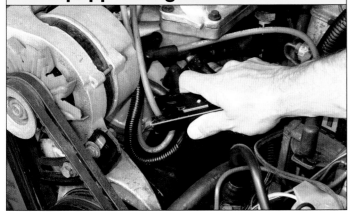

To start the ignition timing check, the timing light is connected to the battery and the spark plug wire for the number-1 cylinder.

12 Aim Timing Light

With the engine idling, the timing light is aimed toward the crankshaft pulley and the fixed timing tab near it.

13 Check Timing

The strobe of the timing light will "freeze" the rotating indicator mark on the pulley, the position of which is compared to the fixed timing tab. In this photo, the timing tab has marks for top dead center (TDC) and degree marks for advanced (BC) and retarded (AC). When the pulley's mark is in sync with the mark (10 degrees, for example) noted in the service manual, the timing is correct.

14 Adjust Timing

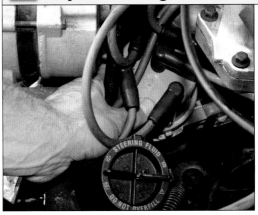

If the ignition timing requires adjustment, loosen the distributor and turn it in slight increments to align the timing marks, when viewed with the timing light. The procedure brings the timing into specification. This means the entire body of the distributor is turned, not only the distributor cap. Only slight rotation of the distributor should be needed.

15 Confirm Timing Adjustment with Timing Light

When a distributor adjustment is made, it is checked with the timing light. As soon as the timing marks align, the adjustment is complete; the timing is set and the distributor is re-tightened. It is very important to avoid moving or jostling the distributor before it is re-tightened, because it could throw off the newly adjusted timing.

Trouble-Shooting Guide

If your engine doesn't roll over or start up as expected, check against the following:

- Vehicle has electrical power, but nothing happens when the key is turned: If the starter solenoid doesn't even make its characteristic "click-click-click" sound when the key is turned, check that the engine-to-chassis ground strap is attached.
- Battery is fully charged and starter relay clicks, but engine does not turn over: Assuming the starter was functional before the rebuild process, check the cable between the starter and relay. Also check the power lead that typically slides on over a post on the relay assembly.
- Clanging sound heard when turning over the engine: The starter may not be correctly aligned on the flywheel/flexplate.
- Engine turns over, but very slowly, as if battery is almost dead: Check for correct and adequate grounds between the engine and body or from the negative battery cable.
- Engine turns over vigorously, but won't start: Check the connection between the distributor and the coil. If the condition is accompanied by a fuel odor, check the fuel line connections.
- Engine starts, but quickly stalls, pops, or seems to be running on less than all cylinders: Check the ignition timing. The distributor may be installed in the wrong position or, if the distributor hold-down was not sufficiently tightened, the distributor may have moved, which would drastically affecting timing.
- Engine starts but runs poorly—rough, stumbling, and with the odor of raw fuel: First check the connections at the mass air sensor and/or MAP sensor; the MAP sensor connection may be a vacuum line from the firewall. If those connections check out, the ignition timing may be off significantly and require the removal of the distributor to correct the timing.

- Engine starts but oil pressure gauge reads low or oil light won't turn off: Turn off the engine immediately. Check that the gauge lead is connected at the oil pressure sending unit on the cylinder block. Clean the connection, if necessary. If the gauge connection appears fine, there may be a problem with the oil pump or a blockage in the oil delivery circuit. In either case, *do not* continue running the engine until the condition is rectified.
- Engine runs and oil pressure is good, but ticking sound heard from engine: On engines with hydraulic lifters, one or more of the lifters may not have "pumped up" fully with oil. This condition may go away relatively quickly. If it doesn't, the lifters may require inspection and/or removal. On non-hydraulic engines, the valve lash may need adjustment.
- Engine heats up, but electric cooling fan doesn't start or coolant doesn't move out of the radiator: On systems with an electric fan, check the wiring connection at the coolant temperature switch; replace the switch if it is old. Also, inspect the thermostat and ensure it has been correctly installed.
- At start-up, coolant/water pours out of the bottom of the water pump: The incorrect water pump gasket was likely installed. Some gasket replacement kits include multiple versions for different model years of the same engine (this is extremely common on Ford 302/ 5.0-liter engines). Remove the water pump and gasket and install the correct gasket.
- Engine runs, but cuts-out or misses when revved: On engines with a distributor, check the ignition wires and leads between the distributor

and coil; make sure none of the spark plug wires are touching one another or getting overheated if resting on the exhaust manifolds. On distributorless engines, check that the crankshaft position sensor is installed correctly and/or the coil lead is connected correctly.

- Engine runs, but the "Check Engine" light is on: Check the exhaust system's oxygen sensor connections first; a neglected oxygen sensor connection will cause the engine light to illuminate immediately. After that, check to ensure all the other electrical connections are hooked up and that there are no air leaks around the air intake system or vacuum leaks from broken or unconnected vacuum lines. If these inspections check out, you may need a plug-in diagnostic tool to check the engine controller for the trouble signal/code, which is causing the Check Engine light to illuminate.

Road Test and Break-In Period

The road test and final inspection are the final steps in the project. They are the most important, as they can determine whether a freshly rebuilt and installed engine will have a long, trouble-free life under the hood.

16 Test Drive

The test drive is an important part of the project because it is integral to the engine's break-in and gives the builder a real-world opportunity to check the engine's operational status.

17 Follow Manufacturer's Recommended Procedure

During the test drive, the engine shouldn't be subjected to full-throttle or high-load conditions. Some manufacturers recommend keeping the engine below a prescribed RPM level for the first few hundred miles. If the builder does not follow these recommendations, engine damage could occur.

18 Check Climate System

The climate system should be engaged during the test drive to ensure the air conditioning system was re-connected correctly. Also, turning on the heater will help circulate coolant more quickly through the engine.

Important!

19 Vary Test Drive Route

The test drive route should include a mix of highway and stop-and-go city-style driving, giving the engine the opportunity to operate throughout the RPM band. This allows the piston rings to seat properly and helps other components break-in with different loads.

Logically, the road test shouldn't be attempted before the engine has been checked for leaks and is filled adequately with coolant. In fact, bring a quart or two of oil and a gallon of pre-mixed coolant for the vehicle's maiden voyage; this may help save the engine that might otherwise be lost to an innocent mistake, such as an oil filter that wasn't sufficiently tightened.

Different engines have different requirements, but most engines should be broken in lightly for the first few hundred miles of service. This means the driver should refrain from heavy-load, full-throttle operation until the engine is broken in adequately. It also means that trailer towing should be avoided for the first 500 miles, or so, of a new engine's life.

The reasons for the light-duty break-in procedures have to do with ensuring proper piston-ring seating and, in some engines, camshaft break-in. The piston rings will bite into the cylinder walls slightly and high engine load early in the engine's life can cause premature ring wear, piston-wall scoring—both of which can cause oil burning and/or consumption—or, worst of all, broken piston rings.

A Half-Hour Drive

When it's time to take the vehicle for its first drive with the rebuilt engine, plan to spend at least 20 minutes to a half-hour driving it. The route should provide some stop-and-go driving and highway speeds; avoid sustained, steady-speed driving. The varied route gives all of the engine's systems the opportunity to function as designed. Simply taking the vehicle onto a freeway for a half-hour may not allow the engine to cycle up and down through its powerband. It may not even allow the cooling fans to kick on in some vehicles.

The test drive should be performed with the radio off, and the driver should pay close attention to the following:

Coolant temperature: Keep an eye on the temperature gauge to make sure the temperature is normal. If the engine seems to run warm, there may not be enough coolant in the system. Conversely, an engine that doesn't seem to come up to temperature may have a thermostat that is stuck in the open position or a cooling fan that turned on prematurely. It may also be do to a replacement thermostat that was too "cold" for the engine (a lower-temperature thermostat) and the engine control computer won't allow the engine to switch to the "open loop" management mode.

Oil pressure: The oil pressure gauge should read higher when the engine is started, but settle down after a few minutes of operation. If the gauge readout shows too-low pressure at start-up or drops severely after a few minutes, stop the vehicle as soon as possible to prevent engine damage. A problem with the gauge would likely manifest itself as no pressure reading whatsoever, so a very low-pressure reading likely indicates an oiling system issue to be resolved.

Amp meter: A seemingly trivial detail, but if the alternator was not correctly re-connected during the assembly process, it may not be charging the battery, and battery power alone may not be enough to get the vehicle home from the test drive.

Heater: After a few minutes of warm-up, the heater should be turned on to check it is operating correctly. The heat should be warm and constant. Heat that is sporadic or that cools briefly before returning again likely indicates air in the cooling system. If this is the case, the cooling system should be carefully opened and allowed to "burp" itself, while more coolant is added to fill the system.

Air conditioning: Like the heater, the air conditioning system should be turned on to check its operation. If the system wasn't discharged during the rebuilding process, it should operate as it did prior to the project. If the cooling performance is spotty, with periods of warm air blowing, a leak has probably developed in the system. Most likely, it is a line that was bent or deformed during the engine removal process. If the A/C system was discharged during the removal stage and recharged after the engine's installation, inadequate performance likely indicates an insufficient amount of refrigerant was added to the system and it should be topped off.

Squeaks, squeals, and other sounds: Listen intently for the sounds of belt squeaks or squeals that could indicate improperly tensioned belts. This condition could also cause low readings on some gauges or a warmer-than-normal engine temperature because a loose or slipping belt isn't turning the water pump at the correct speed.

Other under-hood squeaks could indicate the rubbing of some components that should be better separated. Also, don't discount the possibility of a faulty new part. A new water pump, for example, could have a bad bearing, and if all the other sources of a squeak have been eliminated, a bad new water pump could be the culprit.

Odors: There shouldn't be any surprising odors emanating from under the hood during the test drive. Unless oil or coolant has been spilled on the engine during filling, the driver should smell neither on a properly prepped engine. If the odor of either is detected, it indicates a leak. Pull over immediately and determine the source of the leak.

Engine paint sprayed on the exhaust manifolds or other high-temperature areas could burn off and cause an odor, but it should be brief and disappear by the end of the test drive.

Vehicles equipped with a new clutch kit should not generate an odor from the clutch. If a strong clutch odor is detected, it is likely due to an incorrectly installed clutch or the driver's slipping of the new clutch, perhaps from the unfamiliar feel of the new clutch.

Back Home

If the test drive was successful, with no problems detected, the driver should immediately open the hood and inspect the engine for leaks or other obvious problems. The cooling system should be checked, too. It may have to be topped off, but care must be taken to avoid spilling very hot coolant if the coolant cannot be added to an overflow reservoir. In this case, you should let the engine cool for an hour or so before attempting to open the pressurized cooling system.

First Oil Change

Opinions vary on when it is appropriate to give a rebuilt engine its first oil-and-filter change, but a good general rule is 300 to 500 miles (approximately 500 to 800 km). Check the factory service manual for a specific recommendation. If none exists, follow the 300-mile rule.

The reason for the quick oil change is the likelihood that small metal particles dislodged in the engine during break-in, particularly from the cylinder walls; the oil change allows the engine to be flushed of them. After that, the next oil change should come after approximately 1,000–2,000 more miles have been added to the engine. From there, the regular oil-change schedule should be followed.

Synthetic Oil from the Start?

Since super-slippery synthetic oil hit the market, there have been myths and opinions about when it is most appropriate to use it in a fresh engine. Some insist that the oil is so good at reducing friction that it prevents the piston rings from seating

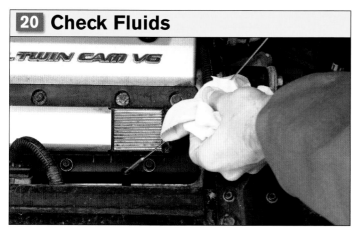

20 Check Fluids

When the test drive is over, the oil level should be checked and topped off, if necessary. The oil on the dipstick should also be inspected for any signs of possible trouble, such as coolant in the oil or metal shavings. The presence of coolant could indicate a head gasket problem, while metal shavings could indicate a variety of issues. If the engine appears to run fine, but metal shavings are in the oil, change the oil immediately and another test drive should be conducted. If the shavings persist after the second test drive, the builder should not continue driving the vehicle until the source of the shavings is determined.

21 Top Off Cooling System

It is likely the cooling system will require an additional quantity of coolant after the test drive. It can be added immediately to vehicles equipped with an overflow/filling reservoir; if the vehicle doesn't have such a reservoir, the builder should wait until the engine has cooled before opening the pressurized cap on the radiator.

during the break-in period. This myth has generally been debunked, particularly because some high-performance engines come from the factory filled with synthetic oil. Generally speaking, synthetic oil may require a slightly longer period for the rings to seat, but they'll seat nonetheless.

I don't suggest using synthetic during the break-in for one simple reason: Economics. Synthetic oil can

22 Synthetic Oil

In most cases, synthetic oil shouldn't be used during the break-in period, as it will typically extend the time it takes for the piston rings to seat. *Some manufacturers have no recommendation on this, while others are very specific—when it doubt, the service manual should be consulted.*

23 Enjoy the Drive

With the pride of a job well done and no leaks, noises, or odors to worry about, the builder can enjoy the fruits of his or her labor with a satisfying drive in the re-powered car. The first oil change should take place around the 300-mile mark; after that, the manufacturer's recommended maintenance schedule can be followed.

cost up to four times the amount of conventional motor oil and, given the 300-mile recommendation for the first oil change, it makes little sense to run very expensive oil through an engine for a comparatively short period.

For those who plan to run synthetic oil in their rebuilt engine, I recommend starting with it *after* the first oil change. You may allow the rings to seat a little quicker and you'll definitely save money. Also, some manufacturers recommend not using synthetic for a prescribed period while the engine is being broken in. It's a good idea to check the owner's manual or service manual for any notes regarding this.

Professional Tuning and Emissions Considerations

If the test drive and break-in period proceed without problems, the engine and vehicle are ready for daily use. Owners in some areas, however, will have to contend with emissions testing. If the engine was rebuilt to factory specifications, including over-bored cylinders and the consequently larger-diameter pistons, the engine should have no trouble in meeting the mandated local emissions requirements. Still, it is not a bad idea to have the vehicle tested after a couple of months of operation. Testing during the break-in period isn't recommended because emissions may be greater while the piston rings seat themselves in the cylinders.

A confirmation of the vehicle's operating condition can be performed at a professional shop that can plug in a diagnostic scanner and check for trouble codes that could indicate an unforeseen problem. Some high-performance-oriented shops have a chassis dynamometer that can be used to measure horsepower and torque output, while also assessing the general tune of the engine. Such test sessions generally start at about $100 and go up from there, but they can provide valuable information as well as a confirmation that your project was, indeed, a success.

Professional Mechanic Tip PRO TIP

24 Chassis Dyno Testing

PRO TIP *A professional tuning shop can provide an extra measure of assurance by checking the vehicle's computer for trouble codes, while performance shops equipped with a chassis dynamometer can measure the engine's power output and general state of tune.*

REMANUFACTURED ENGINES, CRATE ENGINES AND PERFORMANCE UPGRADES

There are instances when the plan of an engine rebuild project goes astray. For some, a cylinder block and/or cylinder heads are unusable for the rebuild. For others, the lure of building a high-horsepower engine becomes too strong to resist. This chapter explores the reasons and options for deviating from a stock-type rebuild of the original engine.

Remanufactured Engines

A remanufactured engine, or "reman," offers an interesting and sometimes cost-effective alternative to rebuilding the original engine. In some instances, it is the *only* alternative for an engine that has suffered irreparable damage to the cylinder block and/or reciprocating assembly. Determining whether the original engine is usable or a reman is required is a decision that occurs during the engine's disassembly and/or the machine shop stages of the project.

Companies obtain engine cores and remanufacture them for rebuilding. Cores are sourced from salvaged vehicles and warranty returns from the OE manufacturer. In some cases, remanufactured engines are available from the original manufacturer. Reman engines are typically built in production line-type settings, so the remanufactured engine obtained for a vehicle will not likely be the original engine removed from the vehicle. This can be a problem for some vehicle owners, particularly those whose vehicles may hold collector value. But an original engine that is damaged beyond repair is not going to power the car anyway, so compromises are inevitable.

Remanufactured engines can offer some advantages. In some cases, the cost can be less than following through with a do-it-yourself rebuild. Also, common problems inherent to an engine line—crack-prone pistons or weak cylinder head bolts, for example—are often solved

during the remanufacturing process. Apart from these upgrades to fix factory flaws, remanufactured engines are built to the same specifications as the factory-original engines.

Most remanufactured engines come in long-block form, meaning they are complete with an assembled reciprocating assembly and cylinder heads, but minus the "take-off" parts that can be re-used from the original engine, such as the intake manifold, front dress, power accessories, and the like.

One of the largest engine remanufactures is Indiana-based JASPER Engine and Transmissions (jasperengines.com), which builds approximately 75,000 gasoline engines every year. Although there are variances among the different remanufactures, JASPER's basic process serves as a guide to what to expect from a reman engine and what to ask before ordering such an engine from any source. They include:

- All-new pistons; not reconditioned originals.
- Cylinder head surfacing; performed to ensure accurate, leak-free sealing.
- Cylinders bored and honed according to OEM specifications.
- Crankshafts with machined journals, fillets, and thrust surfaces.

- All-new valves, valvesprings, and retainers; no reconditioned originals for these high-wear parts.
- Live testing; after the engine is built, it is started and tested before released for sale.

Another alternative to a reman engine may be locating a matching engine from a salvaged vehicle, but it can take time to find a correctly matching engine, and there are usually no guarantees about its condition. And, in addition to the cost of purchasing the salvage engine, it will likely require many of the same rebuilding tasks required for the original engine. It may ultimately cost a few dollars less to recondition

For a catastrophic engine problem that eliminates the possibility of a rebuild, the remanufactured engine is likely the best choice. It is built to the same specifications as the original and carries a guarantee, which may not come with a salvage-yard engine.

Remanufactured engines undergo most of the same processes used in the engine rebuilding process, including machine work such as boring and honing.

Like a rebuilt engine, a remanufactured engine typically receives new pistons, but it retains reconditioned rods and crankshaft.

Unless the manufacturer recommends replacing them, the cylinder heads are re-used on remanufactured engines, although they are typically surfaced.

a salvage engine, but for those with an unsalvageable original engine, a reman could prove to be the cost-effective and time-effective choice for re-powering their vehicle.

Crate Engines

Crate engines are complete, pre-built engine assemblies that are largely ready for immediate installation, much like the remanufactured engines mentioned above. However, crate engines from OEM sources are usually *brand new* engines and not remanufactured from used engine cores. The term crate engine is derived from the typical wooden crate in which the engine is delivered from the manufacturer. They are generally ordered through a dealership parts department or an authorized OEM distributor. Indeed, direct-replacement crate engines are largely interchangeable with a remanufactured engine in the ways they are purchased, delivered, and installed. Not all crate engines are OEM or all-new, however, as non-OEM aftermarket builders offer crate engine packages based on rebuilt or reconditioned cores.

Because OEM crate engines are all-new engines with all-new parts, they generally cost more than remans. And as the case with remanufactured engines, the installation of a crate engine—even one from the vehicle's original manufacturer—means the vehicle is powered by something other than its original engine. For most owners or builders, this should be of little concern.

In addition to crate engines built to production specifications, many OEM manufacturers offer performance-upgraded crate engines that deliver more horsepower and/or torque than the original engine. Although more expensive than original-spec crate engines, these high-performance crate engines offer the benefit of a pre-tested performance combination. In other words, there's no guesswork trying to select higher-performance cylinder heads, camshafts, and other items; all this work has been done.

The caveat with high-performance crate engines is the effect they have on the vehicle's engine control computer. Most of these electronic controllers are designed to operate within specific parameters, and the introduction of an engine that has different air-fuel needs can cause operational difficulty. Some vehicles require costly controller calibration updates to deliver smooth, trouble-free operation. This isn't the case with every high-performance crate engine, but it should be considered and investigated before installing such an engine in a later-model, computer-controlled vehicle. Even older vehicles predating modern electronic controls will encounter issues, if the high-performance crate engine does not accommodate the original-type emissions controls.

Installing a Crate Engine: A Case Study

Typical of an enthusiast looking for a little more towing power from his truck, which is used for pulling a large camper, truck owner Leonard Slebodnik turned to an OEM crate engine to answer his needs. Slebodnik's truck was a 1999 Chevy Suburban 4x4 with approximately 100,000 miles and a 350-ci (5.7-liters) V-8 engine. Rather than rebuilding the original engine or installing a stock-type crate engine, he ordered a replacement engine (383-ci) from General Motors' Performance Parts division (available through GM dealership parts departments) at gmperformanceparts.com.

Officially named the HT383E (GM part number 17800393), it was designed as a direct, emissions-legal replacement for the 350-ci engine in certain 1996–1999 GM trucks. As a bonus, it delivered more horsepower and torque—just what Slebodnik was looking for to flatten out some of the hills while towing. It came as a complete assembly, minus the intake and accessory items specific to the Suburban. The basic installation steps are illustrated in this chapter, but it should be noted that the procedures are essentially the same for the installation of a remanufactured engine.

The old engine was removed and technician Nick Schmidt, along with some extra hands, installed the new 383-ci engine. The truck was running by the end of two business days. That is a remarkable turnaround time, as the engine rebuilding process takes much longer. The relative speed of installing a crate engine mitigates the considerable expense of buying an all-new engine, too. Despite that, rebuilding the original engine would have been much less expensive.

Still, Slebodnik got what he wanted: an OEM-tested, high-performance engine that was easy to order, purchase, and have installed. What was notably impressive about the HT383E was the completeness of the package. It came fully assembled, including cylinder heads, water pump, balancer, and even the spark plugs. Additionally, a new distributor was included, along with new intake manifold gaskets, exhaust manifold gaskets, and other odds and ends.

The HT383E was claimed to work with the vehicle's factory computer without additional calibrations, but it was found that additional calibration enhanced its performance and drivability. Removing and replacing the 350 V-8 was mostly straightforward; once the original engine was out of the vehicle, it didn't take long to swap over the intake manifold, pulleys, and exhaust manifolds to the new 383. Then, the new engine was hoisted back over the engine bay and slowly lowered.

As smooth as the procedure was, a few items, that weren't surprising on a truck of this vintage, required additional work and/or replacements. Schmidt installed a new starter, new serpentine belt, and a few other items that, on a 100,000-mile truck, represented insurance as much as necessary replacements.

After the 383-ci engine was installed in the truck, the timing was set, and the oil system primed, it immediately fired up and idled smoothly. Schmidt followed the break-in procedure outlined in the manual supplied with the engine. After about 300 break-in miles, the truck was put on a chassis dyno, and the results showed clear gains across the board, with more horsepower and torque to the tires.

While the truck performed with a noticeable improvement over the stock, worn engine, the results could have been better. It was determined that the stock exhaust system was inadequate for the higher-performance 383-ci engine, and some calibration work would optimize overall performance. After all, the stock computer was still operating under the impression that it was controlling the stock 350-ci engine. The camshaft profile of the 383, as well as the air-fuel requirements, differed from the 350, and the controller was working to keep the engine operating at the levels for the original engine. Slebodnik reports the engine idles lower than the original 350, but that is the only notable difference in drivability. This would not have been an issue with a stock-type direct-replacement engine.

Nevertheless, the project proved the viability of a drop-in crate engine. The shop's turnaround time was very quick, and the owner, Slebodnik, was back on the road quicker than if he'd gone with a traditional engine rebuild. It may not be the option or desire for all, but the crate engine option is one to seriously consider.

Performance Tip

Crate Engines

The term "crate engine" has a very obvious root. Most are packaged and delivered in large wooden crates. Unless the your home shop is equipped with a forklift, a shop crane will be needed to move the engine around after it is delivered.

A GM Performance Parts HT383E crate engine is designed as a direct replacement for the 350-ci (5.7L) engine of countless 1996–1999

GM pickups and full-size SUVs with the Vortec engines. The HT383E (part number 17800393) is a 50-state emissions-legal replacement crate engine and comes complete. The assembly includes the water pump, distributor, balancer, and spark plugs. Basically, the old engine donates its intake manifold/throttle body assembly and vehicle-specific accessories (this photo shows one of the accessory brackets already transferred to the crate engine).

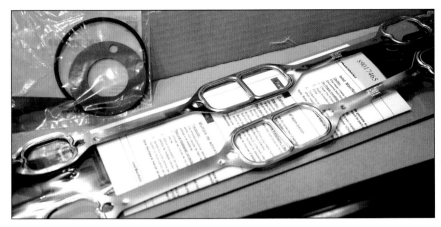

The crate engine package also came with many of the support parts needed to complete the transfer of components from the original engine, including gaskets and seals. It even came with a brand-new distributor.

1 Crate Engine Installation Procedure

Like any engine swap, the process begins with the removal of accessories and components that would otherwise impede the removal of the engine. Technician Nick Schmidt digs into the project Chevy Suburban, draining the fluids, and disconnecting the various supporting components from the engine.

With the engine stripped down, attention turns to extraction. Here, a hoist chain is connected to the engine via factory lift points, including a bracket mounted to the front corner of the block. Note, too, the rag stuffed into the throttle body, which prevents debris from falling into the intake manifold.

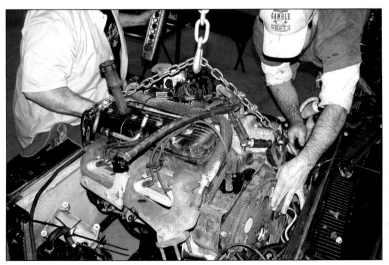

The tried and true 350 served well for about 100,000 miles of work. It was still in good condition, but starting to suffer from a few typical Vortec V-8 afflictions, including warped intake manifold gaskets. A rebuild would have brought the engine back to original condition, but the Suburban's owner wanted more power for towing a camper trailer.

2 Engine Extraction

Here's the Suburban's original 5.7-liter (350-cubic-inch) small-block engine extracted from the chassis. Pulling the engine required the removal of the truck's hood. The process of removal was the same as outlined in Chapter 2, but worn and cracked oil cooler lines added to the disconnection/disassembly chores.

After being removed from the engine, the transferred components received a bath in the parts cleaner. There's no sense putting grimy parts on a shiny, new engine. Gasket residue also was cleaned off the parts destined for transfer to the crate engine, thereby preventing leaks that could occur at start-up or, worse, a few hundred miles after the installation.

3 Component Transfer

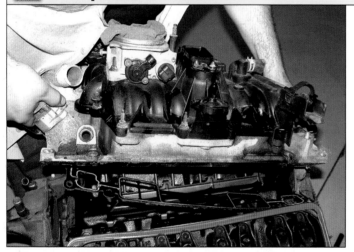

The cleaned-up intake manifold was dropped on to the 383 to begin the final assembly of the engine. In this instance, the valve covers of the new engine required removal for a snag-free installation of the manifold.

With the old engine out, attention turned to removing the components that would be transferred to the 383 crate engine, including the intake manifold. Other re-used parts from the original engine included the front accessories, brackets, and pulleys, as well as the exhaust manifolds and starter. The 383-ci crate engine came with a new distributor and a complete gasket set.

Important details such as the installation of temperature sensors and emissions equipment also are taken care of while the engine is out of the vehicle.

4 Sensor Details

5 Ready for Installation

Important!

Here's the HT383E with all of the necessary components transferred and installed. It was a simple series of procedures that didn't take very long to complete, but attention to detail was needed to ensure no sensors, hoses, or other components were neglected in the transfer and build-up of the crate engine.

6 Drop in Crate Engine

Important!

Carefully, the new 383 is lowered into the engine compartment. It generally takes some refinement to ensure the engine seats properly on the frame and lines up correctly with the transmission. This means ensuring the engine is level and sits correctly on the chassis mounting points. It is also crucial to line up the engine with the transmission to ensure easy fastener installation.

7 Install Exhaust Manifolds

The final step before hoisting the engine up for installation in the vehicle was the installation of exhaust manifolds. After 100,000 miles of heat-up/cool-down expansion and contraction, they may require the use of a manifold spreader to align with the bolt holes. Fortunately, these didn't.

8 Hardware Connections

With the engine bolted down in the chassis, work turns to re-connecting myriad hoses, electrical connectors, and accessories. Here, the throttle cable is connected to the throttle body.

9 Fill Engine with Fluids

With all the hoses connected, the engine is filled with fluids in preparation for the initial start. Priming the oil system, too, is required with most crate engines prior to starting the engine.

Critical Inspection

10 Installation Completed

Here's the installed 383-ci crate engine. Ignition timing was set according to the instruction manual and the engine was started. It fired up on the first try and ran briefly before being turned off so that installer Nick Schmidt could check for leaks and perform a general inspection. Luckily, the shop floor beneath our truck remained dry.

Performance Tip

11 Break-In Crate Engine

The break-in procedure for the engine was followed by putting a couple hundred light-duty miles on it. Then, the engine was treated to an oil change and another inspection. The Suburban was also put on a chassis dynamometer to confirm the seat-of-the-pants feel in increased horsepower.

A few more break-in miles are needed before the newly empowered truck should tow a trailer. The best aspect of the project was the truck running with its new engine within two days of the project's start. That simply can't be done with a traditional engine rebuild.

High-Performance Parts

It is an instinct that emerges during an engine rebuild project: building in greater performance. It's a temptation that can easily lead to a better-performing vehicle. It can also be a slippery slope, down which lots of money is lost and that results in a vehicle with either negligible performance gains or, worse, deteriorated drivability.

The focus of this book has been on the fundamentals of removing, rebuilding, and reinstalling an engine, but it's impossible to ignore the draw of adding on components or systems that enhance performance. After all, with the engine out of the vehicle and torn apart, there is no better opportunity to add high-performance parts. That said, this section does not delve too deeply into the theories involved and man-

ners in which to build high-performance engines. CarTech has dozens of book titles dedicated to those very topics, but this section will outline some of the more basic and popular "bolt on" performance-enhancing modifications.

There are countless methods of building power, ranging from the cost-neutral to the wildly expensive, and from the very easy to the outrageously intricate. For those performing the stock-type rebuild outlined throughout this book, the cost-neutral, inexpensive, and bolt-on upgrades will likely be of most interest. Again, if you're looking for instructions on combustion chamber bowl blending or supercharger installations, try one of CarTech's other books.

Cost-neutral performance upgrades are those that involve replacement parts that are already

required for the engine rebuild, such as the camshaft. Inexpensive and bolt-on items include upgrades and/or replacement parts for components that don't necessarily require replacement during the rebuild process. Examples of this would include valvetrain rocker arms and exhaust manifolds.

Here's a look at some general performance upgrades and what to consider with them:

Camshaft

A camshaft with more lift and/or duration than stock enables the engine to make more power. If the camshaft(s) requires replacement during the rebuild, it is simple to order a "hotter" cam. However, camshafts are dependent on their relationship with the valvetrain for optimal performance, so replacing a cam may also require changing the valvesprings

---

Performance Tip

Camshaft Consideration

A "hotter" camshaft that delivers greater lift and/or duration can significantly improve an engine's performance. It can add horsepower, torque, and (perhaps) extend the effective RPM range. The builder should consult with the camshaft manufacturer prior to ordering, to make sure the new cam will work well with the rest of the engine combination.

Performance Tip

Valvetrain Upgrades

One of the concerns when upgrading the camshaft is its effect on the valvetrain. Too much lift can be incompatible with the stock valvesprings and/or rocker arms. Again, researching the best option with the cam manufacturer will reveal whether new valvesprings and/or rocker arms are needed to match the hotter camshaft.

---

and/or rocker arms. Cams can also affect the idle quality and vacuum output of the engine, leading in some cases to diminished drivability or weaker brake performance. The key is to pick a performance cam that has been matched to the engine. Most cam manufacturers have applications for specific engine combinations, which minimize the chance of drivability issues. In other words, there may be an off-the-shelf "hot" camshaft for your specific engine that requires little-to-no additional components or modifications.

Builders of engines with multiple cams will find a performance upgrade more expensive that those engines with a single, cam-in-block design. But, as swapping cams in an overhead-cam engine can be a chore

otherwise, adding hotter cams during the rebuilding process is a cost-effective method of performing the upgrade.

Cylinder Heads

High-performance replacement cylinder heads typically offer greater performance through increased airflow. This is due to larger or reconfigured intake ports, larger valves, or both. Additional benefits can come with the replacement of the original cast-iron cylinder head with lightweight aluminum versions. Aluminum heads can save up to 100 pounds on a typical V-8 engine, but it is a comparatively expensive investment that doesn't necessarily offer a horsepower advantage over a comparable, high-flow iron head.

The addition of performance cylinder heads typically requires the investment of more components, such as a camshaft and intake system. The high airflow capability of performance heads may necessitate more than the stock cam and intake can support. On carbureted engines, this may require a high-flow intake manifold and larger carburetor. On a fuel-injected engine, this may require higher-capacity fuel injectors and perhaps a larger throttle body and/or manifold.

For those who are unfamiliar with assembling cylinder heads and don't have the equipment for it at a home shop, I suggest buying fully assembled heads. Bare heads are less expensive, but they also require the purchase and assembly of the valves, springs, retainers, etc.

Performance Tip

High-Performance Heads

Replacement cylinder heads are available for many popular domestic and import engines. This iron small-block Ford head from World Products, for example, nearly doubles the airflow over the stock heads for relatively little money. Installing the heads during the engine assembly stage saves time and money, too, when compared with an in-vehicle head swap.

Aluminum heads offer a weight advantage, but not necessarily a performance advantage over an iron head with comparably sized intake ports and valve sizes. Iron heads are less expensive.

Performance Tip

Complementing Cylinder Head

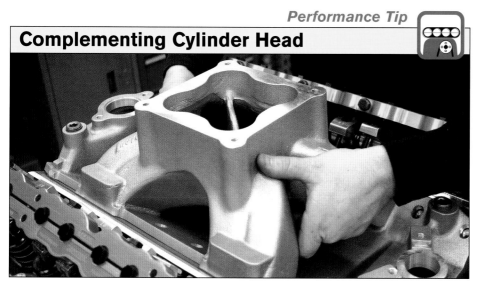

High-performance cylinder heads will likely require the installation of components to support their airflow capability, such as an upgraded intake and carburetor and, perhaps, a high-performance camshaft.

Cam and Head Combination

For many popular engines, there are tailored camshaft and cylinder head combinations that include matched high-performance components. Some also include a matched intake manifold. These all-inclusive kits are designed to bolt on to the engine without the need for further modifications. They can cost only a few hundred dollars or more than $2,000, but the cost is mitigated by the fact that the engine already requires assembly; installing such parts on an engine that is already in a vehicle could double the cost invested in the parts themselves. Also, these matched kits eliminate the question of airflow; the components are designed to work together for optimized airflow.

Computer-controlled vehicles likely require revised calibration to deliver smooth, optimized performance. Also, many combinations are emissions-legal but some are not. If smog testing is required in your area, be sure to check the emissions standards of the jurisdiction in which the vehicle will be legally registered before bolting performance parts onto your engine.

Carburetor and Intake Manifold Combination

Carbureted engines can often benefit from an upgraded carburetor and intake manifold set, such as

Performance Tip

Intake Manifold Swap

A replacement intake manifold can provide increased airflow or convert a one- or two-barrel engine to a four-barrel carburetor. Selecting a manifold that is matched to the performance capability and local emissions regulations is the challenge, but for popular engines, there are numerous selections. The aluminum four-barrel intake manifold seen here is for a Pontiac V-8 and is a direct replacement for the heavy, cast-iron original. It offers superior airflow and a significant weight advantage. A matched carburetor with this manifold can greatly improve horsepower and torque.

Performance Tip

Carburetor Change

A builder who is unfamiliar with selecting a carburetor should consult a professional before up-sizing the component, especially when switching from a two-barrel to a four-barrel. Too much carburetor can overwhelm the engine with fuel, particularly at low speeds, causing drivability problems and, perhaps, delivering no real-world performance benefit.

changing from a 2-barrel design to a 4-barrel combination. A swap to an aftermarket aluminum manifold can also save a tremendous amount of weight over original-style cast-iron manifolds. Typically, aluminum aftermarket manifolds have great performance advantage over stock units, probably requiring a larger-capacity carburetor.

However, it is very easy to "over-carb" an engine, effectively ruining its performance and drivability. In fact, some engines will not respond positively to a larger carburetor. Also, the emissions equipment compatibility is a significant detail to consider, as well as emissions legality once the engine is back in the vehicle. The bottom line is: The engine builder should check carefully for components matched to his or her engine.

If you consider such a change, you should seek a matched combination or consult with a vendor, such as Edelbrock or Holley, to ensure optimized parts are selected. Both companies offer many packages tailored to specific engine combinations. Many of these kits are also emissions-legal, carrying the requisite CARB (California Air Resources Board) certification for use in California and the other states that follow California's emissions regulations.

There are also replacement performance manifolds for fuel-injected engines that use TBI-type systems; mostly these are 1980s and early 1990s-style GM V-8 engines.

Rocker Arms

Numerically higher-ratio rocker arms (used on overhead-valve engines) can provide a noticeable horsepower gain for little extra money. Higher-ratio rockers effectively act like a small bump in camshaft lift, and they are very easy to install. However, they represent an additional expense over the cost of the basic engine rebuild, as the stock rocker arms are typically reused. Still, they are relatively inexpensive to purchase and can generally add anywhere from 5 to 15 horsepower.

Another benefit of higher-ratio rocker arms is the fact that they don't require any other modifications or turning to be effective. There are many rocker arm kits available for popular engines. For example, SLP Performance Parts, in Toms River, New Jersey, is a specialist in late-model GM V-8 engines and offers a wide array of rocker arm kits for LS-type GM engines.

Exhaust Headers/Manifolds

One of the oldest and most proven methods of building power is the use of higher-flow exhaust headers or manifolds. Because they can be difficult to install on some vehicles, particularly on front-drive vehicles that "hide" a side of the engine from easy access, installing them while the engine is out of the vehicle makes the task much easier. Replacement headers can cost several hundred dollars, but can offer a significant increase in performance. In fact, if other airflow-enhancing modifications have been made to the engines, such as a new camshaft, intake, or cylinder heads, headers should be considered almost mandatory. This is because the increased airflow through the engine can be restricted at the less-efficient stock exhaust manifolds.

Higher-Ratio Rockers

Numerically higher-ratio rocker arms can provide the equivalent of an increase in camshaft lift. In most cases, these are a direct bolt-on replacement. They can be added during the engine assembly and generally require no other complementing modifications.

Performance Tip

Valvetrain Upgrades

In this photo, the slight changes in rocker arm ratios are shown at the oil hole located at the top of each part, and this demonstrates the fulcrum variance between them. It is a slight difference, but often effective enough to add several horsepower.

Headers

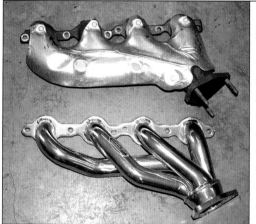

Performance Tip

Exhaust headers replace stock exhaust manifolds and offer increased flow for improved performance. Headers are generally lighter in weight than conventional cast-iron exhaust manifolds. Here, a stock manifold for a GM V-8 truck engine is contrasted with a replacement header from SLP Performance Parts.

Headers help improve flow out of the engine, allowing it to make the most of its new performance parts.

Care should be taken to avoid bulky headers that may interfere with the installation of the engine. Also, seek headers or manifolds that bolt up to the stock exhaust/catalytic converter system; some headers are longer than the stock manifolds, requiring all-new exhaust components after the headers.

Larger Throttle Body

Another highly popular bolt-on performance upgrade is a larger throttle body for port-injected engines. This means the inlet bore diameter(s) is larger than stock and allows ingestion of more air into the intake manifold. These parts are relatively cheap and easy to install, but they may not enable more horsepower if the engine is otherwise stock. Generally, a fuel-injected engine's airflow is carefully controlled and simply allowing for more air doesn't mean the computer will allow the engine to make the most of it. In some cases, no discernable performance or drivability difference will be noted, while in others the larger throttle body may cause low-speed stumbling or other drivability issues without proper tuning or computer calibrations.

A larger throttle body, like adding a larger capacity carburetor, must also be matched to other airflow-enhancing modifications, such as high-performance heads and a camshaft. In other words, a larger throttle body on an otherwise-stock engine will do little good. It is also probable that tuning or computer recalibration will be required once the new throttle body is installed, because the computer will have to be told to work with the added airflow—this is also the case for computer-controlled engines with new heads or a hotter camshaft.

Computer Calibrations

Cars and trucks of the last 25 years or so with fuel-injected engines have engine-control computers, known as the electronic control module (ECM) or powertrain control module (PCM) that strictly regulates the operation of the engine. This generally means controlling the fuel delivery and airflow to match programmed parameters. Increasing the airflow of the engine, such as with high-flow heads, brings a requisite need for increased fuel, but without new calibrations, the engine will continue to supply fuel at the pre-programmed rate. Too little fuel to match the airflow results in a lean condition that could damage the engine or cause outright failure.

Builders who upgrade their computer-controlled engine with airflow-enhancing performance parts must take the proper tuning into account to ensure safe engine operation. This

Performance Tip

High-Flow Throttle Body

A throttle body with larger-diameter bores allows the engine to draw in more air, but it should only be added if the engine is equipped to push more air through its passages, such as with high-flow heads and/or a higher-lift camshaft.

Controller Upgrade

Proper engine controller tuning or calibration is a must for computer-controlled engines equipped with performance parts. The computer must be "told" about the increased airflow capability in order to match it with fuel and ignition timing. Hand-held programmers, such as the one seen here, can provide pre-loaded tuning that can be simply uploaded to the vehicle's computer.

is typically done after the engine is installed in the vehicle and reconnected to the ECM or PCM. On some vehicles, the calibration requires the attention of a professional, who will upload a custom program to the computer. Some systems can utilize mail-order calibrations, whereby a custom-programmed "chip" is sent to you for a relatively simple plug-in procedure.

Some later-model vehicles can benefit from hand-held, do-it-yourself programmers that enable you to upload a custom program that was pre-loaded on the device. Often, these programmers accompany a performance upgrade kit, such as rocker arms and a camshaft. The manufacturer supplies the programmer with the optimized tune required for the engine to run with the new parts. This is a very easy solution, but it is not yet available for many vehicles.

Also, there are some engines with very limiting air-fuel control and restrictive computers that virtually disallow engine modifications. The bottom line for builders of later-model, fuel-injected engines is this: Check the tuning or calibration

requirements and availability before proceeding with the purchase of new performance parts. Also, new parts and a revised calibration may affect the emissions of the vehicle, so you should check with the parts manufacturer to ensure the performance components are emissions-legal.

Ignition Upgrade

Ignition technology has made tremendous gains in the past 30 years. The introduction of high-energy-type ignition systems and ignition controllers, such as the popular 6A boxes from MSD and similar competitors, has enabled greater performance, smoother operation, and

better all-around performance. Perhaps the biggest advance was the changeover from breaker points-style distributors to electronic ignitions. And while changing over an engine with a points-type distributor to an electronically controlled distributor is not difficult, there is an inexpensive, very easy method that allows you to retain the engine's original distributor but replace the points with an electronic module.

Such kits are available from a variety of manufacturers, but the most popular and widely recognized points-swap kits are from Pertronix Performance Products (pertronix.com). The swap involves simply removing

Breaker Point Ignition Replacement

The Pertronix Ignitor II ignition kit replaces the breaker points found in distributors with a self-contained electronic module. Start-up, idle, and highway performance are significantly improved with such a conversion, and it eliminates the need for points replacement.

Electronic Ignition Module

Installation of the Pertronix kit starts with the removal of the distributor's breaker point setup. It simply unscrews and pulls off of the distributor base.

The Petronix module takes the place of the points and is connected via a couple of wires to the distributor. It is a very simple, very effective way to enhance the performance and drivability of older vehicles.

the points and replacing them with a drop-in module that is self-contained and requires no additional engine wiring. I have used Pertronix kits on several projects and recommend them; start-up and idle quality is greatly improved in most cases and the installation is very easy. Most kits are priced around $100 or so, making them extremely cost effective.

Chrome Dress-Up Kits

No, shiny parts won't pull any more horsepower out of an engine, but with all of the time and money invested in a rebuilt engine, it doesn't hurt to show it off a bit with a some chrome parts. Many popular engines (mostly V-8s) can be outfitted with chrome kits that include valve covers, an air cleaner, and more. They are generally inexpensive and install just like the original parts; however, you should make sure that any

replacement valve covers include the necessary breather/oil-inlet holes. Also, some chrome air cleaners may not be compatible with all of the emissions equipment of the stock air cleaner.

Chrome Appearance

There's not an easier way to draw attention to a freshly rebuilt engine than with a few polished-chrome engine parts.

WORK-A-LONG SHEET

DISASSEMBLY

Project Statistics

Your Name _____ Today's Date_____

Vehicle Engine Removed From _____ Engine Year _____

CI/L _____ RPO _____

Accessories Attached to Used Engine

❑ A/C Pump ❑ AIR Pump ❑ AIR Lines and Hoses ❑ Water Pump ❑ Flywheel ❑ Clutch ❑ Flexplate

❑ Transmission ❑ Starter ❑ Fuel Rails/Injectors ❑ All Pulleys; Except _____ ❑ Alternator

❑ Coils ❑ Intake Manifold ❑ Exhaust Manifolds ❑ Motor Mounts ❑ Motor Mount Attaching Brackets

❑ Spark Plug Heat Shields ❑ EGR Valve ❑ Dipstick Tube ❑ All Bolts; except _____

❑ _____ ❑ _____ ❑ Items Attached to Intake Manifold (brackets, etc) _____

_____

Operational Notes

Oil consumption _____ Compression check pressure variation _____ psi

Leak-down percent _____ Other observations _____

_____

Disassembly Notations

Head gaskets ❑ MLS ❑ Graphite-layered

Worn/damaged lifters ❑ No ❑ Yes; where _____

Cam sensor location ❑ Rear of block ❑ Front cover

Knock sensor location ❑ Valley ❑ Sides of block

Coolant air bleed pipe style _____

Clutch pilot bearing present ❑ Yes ❑ No

Valve seal/spring seat style ❑ 1-Piece ❑ 2-Piece

Cylinder head plug/sensor locations _____

M11 head bolt style ❑ All-same length ❑ Short/long

Other signs of damage _____

INSPECTION

Initial Parts Inspection Observations

Block OK   ❑ Yes   ❑ No; describe problem _____

Heads OK   ❑ Yes   ❑ No; describe problem _____

Crank OK   ❑ Yes   ❑ No; describe problem _____

Bearings OK   ❑ Yes   ❑ No; describe problem _____

Pistons OK   ❑ Yes   ❑ No; describe problem _____

Cam/lifters OK   ❑ Yes   ❑ No; describe problem _____

Damper OK   ❑ Yes   ❑ No; describe problem _____

Intake manifold OK   ❑ Yes   ❑ No; describe problem _____

Exhaust manifold OK   ❑ Yes   ❑ No; describe problem _____

Oil pump OK   ❑ Yes   ❑ No; describe problem _____

Main cap mating surfaces damage/abnormalities   ❑ No   ❑ Yes

Identifying marks you placed on any parts (Non-intrusive method only!) _____

AT THE MACHINE SHOP

Parts Delivered to the Machine Shop

❑ Block   ❑ Main Caps   ❑ Crankshaft   ❑ Oil Pump   ❑ Oil Pump Pickup   ❑ Connecting Rods

❑ Pistons   ❑ Piston Rings   ❑ Camshaft   ❑ Lifters   ❑ Damper   ❑ Main Bearings

❑ Rod Bearings   ❑ Cam Bearings   ❑ Rod Bolts   ❑ Gasket Set   ❑ Pushrods   ❑ Rocker Arms

❑ Head Bolts   ❑ Main Bolts/Studs   ❑ Miscellaneous Nuts/Bolts/Brackets for Cleaning   ❑ Water Pump

❑ Timing Cover   ❑ Oil Pan   ❑ Flywheel/Flexplate   ❑ Clutch   ❑ Exhaust Manifolds

❑ Motor Mounts   ❑ Motor Mount Attaching Brackets   ❑ Assembled Heads

❑ Disassembled Heads with: ❑ Valves   ❑ Springs   ❑ Retainers   ❑ Keepers

❑ Intake Manifold

❑ _____   ❑ _____   ❑ _____   ❑ _____   ❑ _____

Special Instructions for Machine Shop

❑ Bore block   ❑ Hone block   ❑ Desired piston-to-wall clearance: 0._____-inch   ❑ Grind crank

❑ Desired rod bearing clearance: 0.____-inch   ❑ Desired main bearing clearance: 0.____-inch   ❑ Resurface block

❑ Resurface heads   ❑ Install cam bearings   ❑ Gap piston rings   ❑ Assemble cylinder heads

Is pilot bushing to be installed in crankshaft (required for manual transmission)?   ❑ Yes   ❑ No

After You Pick Up Your Parts

❑ Yes ❑ No   Threaded holes reconditioned/chased   ❑ Yes ❑ No   Cam bearings installed

❑ Yes ❑ No   Plugs installed (coolant/oil gallery)   ❑ Yes ❑ No   Crank keys installed

PRE-ASSEMBLY FITTING

Measured and Recorded During Pre-Assembly Fitting

Measured valvespring installed height:

1 _____   3 _____   5 _____   7 _____

2 _____   4 _____   6 _____   8 _____

Spring shims used to obtain correct installed height:

1 _____ 3 _____ 5 _____ 7 _____

2 _____ 4 _____ 6 _____ 8 _____

Measured valvespring coil bind height _____ -inches

Calculated compressed valvespring clearance:

1 _____ 3 _____ 5 _____ 7 _____

2 _____ 4 _____ 6 _____ 8 _____

Reluctor ring runout OK? ❏ Yes ❏ No   Measured runout of 0. _____ -inch

Crank straightness OK? ❏ Yes ❏ No   Runout on center main of 0. _____ -inch

Main bearing clearance OK? ❏ Yes ❏ No   Measured clearance 0. _____ -inch

Crank thrust OK? ❏ Yes ❏ No   Measured clearance 0. _____ -inch

Camshaft bearing fit OK? ❏ Yes ❏ No;   Describe problem _____

Piston–to-wall clearance OK? ❏ Yes ❏ No   Measured clearance 0. _____ -inch

Pistons with incorrect clearance _____

Measured ring end gap:

1 Top _____ 2nd _____   3 Top _____ 2nd _____   5 Top _____ 2nd _____   7 Top _____ 2nd _____

2 Top _____ 2nd _____   4 Top _____ 2nd _____   6 Top _____ 2nd _____   8 Top _____ 2nd _____

Rod bearing clearance OK? ❏ Yes ❏ No   Measured clearance 0. _____ -inch

Rod side clearance OK? ❏ Yes ❏ No   Measured clearance 0. _____ -inch

Piston-to-head clearance OK? ❏ Yes ❏ No   Measured clearance 0. _____ -inch

Cylinders with incorrect clearance _____

Adjustable crank sprocket keyway used: ❏ + – 2   ❏ + – 4   ❏ + – 6   ❏ + – 8   ❏ + – 10   ❏ + – 12

Rotating assembly clearance OK? ❏ Yes ❏ No;   Cause of interference_____

Rocker geometry OK? ❏ Yes ❏ No;   Describe problem _____

Rocker-to-retainer clearance OK? ❏ Yes ❏ No   Maximum 0. _____ -inch (Intake); 0. _____-inch (Exhaust)

Piston-to-valve clearance OK? ❏ Yes ❏ No   Maximum 0. _____ -inch (Intake); 0. _____ -inch (Exhaust)

Other checks/observations: _____

_____

_____

_____

_____

_____

_____

_____

_____

_____

_____

_____

_____

_____

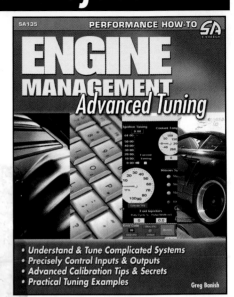
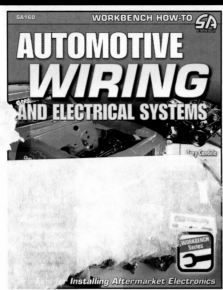

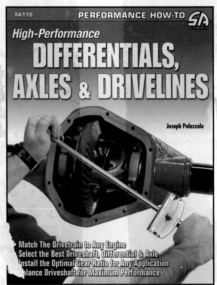